A to Z
OF
Knitting
...
Martingale®
& COMPANY

A to Z of Knitting
© 2006 Country Bumpkin Publications

First published in Australia in 2006 by
Country Bumpkin Publications
916 South Road, Edwardstown
South Australia 5039, Australia
www.countrybumpkin.com.au

Editor: Sue Gardner
Assistant Editor: Lizzie Kulinski
History Section: Susan O'Connor
Design and Layout: Lynton Grandison
Photography: Andrew Dunbar
Illustrations: Kathleen Barac
Publisher: Margie Bauer

Hardcover first published in U.S. in 2007 by
Martingale & Company
19021 120th Ave. NE, Suite 102
Bothell, WA 98011-9511 USA
ShopMartingale.com

Martingale®
& COMPANY

ISBN: 978-1-56477-914-4

Printed in China
17 16 15 14   12 11 10 9

Mission Statement
Dedicated to providing quality products
and service to inspire creativity.

Special thanks to Needle Nook
www.needlenook.com.au

Contents

KNIT [v]
1. *to make (a fabric or garment) by intertwining yarn or thread
in a series of connected loops either by hand, with knitting needles, or on a machine.*
2. *to form (yarn or thread) into fabric by intertwining.*

The History of Knitting

Knitting is not an ancient technique. Unlike other textile crafts such as weaving, which has its origins more than 10,000 years ago, the first known examples of knitting come from around the eighth century. Knitting was, at one stage, thought to date from the third century but these examples have now been identified as *nalbinding*, a single needle technique that was practiced in a number of areas, including Africa and Scandinavia. Nalbinding is similar to knitting in appearance but is worked using a single, eyed needle and short lengths of yarn.

Nalbinding

It is thought that knitting developed from nalbinding when someone realized that new loops could be pulled through existing ones with a hooked rod and a continuous length of yarn could be used. Eventually the hooks were deemed unnecessary and plain knitting rods, as we use today, became standard equipment.

Early examples of knitting were worked in the round with four or five needles and using only a knit stitch. Purl stitches were developed later and were used as decorative stitches. Knitting was used primarily for making socks and stockings, its elastic nature being perfect for this task. It is difficult to determine when knitting on two needles was first done because many early examples of knitting are incomplete pieces and the path of the yarn is indiscernible.

Knitting through the Ages
In the Beginning

Evidence of early knitting is sparse. The materials used, namely wool, cotton, and sometimes silk, are not durable and therefore much has been lost over the years.

The earliest pieces of true hand knitting come from Egypt. Many pieces are difficult to date but there are several examples from around the thirteenth century, mostly richly patterned socks. Some include bands of Arabic script that has been simplified as part of the decoration. Most of these are knitted in cotton.

Fascinating references to knitting from the fourteenth century come from paintings rather than knitted fragments. These paintings, scenes of the Holy Family or Madonna and Child, clearly show the Madonna knitting, usually in the round on four or five needles. In one painting she has almost completed a short-sleeved garment; in another she appears to be knitting a patterned bag. Although the paintings offer little tangible information about knitting, they show that it was well known in both Italy and Germany where the paintings originated.

Knitting was used to create purses for holding the relics of saints in both Switzerland and France in the thirteenth and fourteenth centuries. These drawstring bags were knitted in the round from silk thread and were decorated

Jacket / Italy /
Seventeenth century / Knitted silk thread

with allover patterns or bands of pattern or heraldic symbols. Church knitting was not limited to relic purses. In Europe, there are several examples still in existence of knitted liturgical gloves worked between the thirteenth and sixteenth centuries. These gloves, decorated with embroidery or knitted patterns, were worn by bishops and abbots.

It was also during the thirteenth century that the first evidence of knitting appeared in England, in the form of felted caps that were worn by soldiers and sailors. Knitted from coarse, dark wool on four needles, each cap was then felted and shorn to create a smooth surface. The production of these caps was a profitable business and in 1488 the Capper's Act fixed prices to stop the cappers profiteering from their trade. Examples of knitted caps in varying styles have been found in London, Wales, and Scotland. Some resemble skull caps, are close fitting, and have earflaps, while others are flat with a knitted brim.

Knitting did not readily become a popular method for creating other garments. Much of the reason for this may have been the difficulty in producing quality steel needles. It was not until the sixteenth century that a method for producing fine needles was developed.

The Trade in Knitted Stockings

Like caps, knitted stockings were also produced on a large scale. In England these were made primarily for children until the reign of Elizabeth I, when steel needles became readily available and the popularity of knitting spread throughout the country. The elasticity of

Pair of gloves
Spain / Sixteenth century
Knitted silk and silver
thread in stockinette stitch

knitted fabric makes it perfect for socks and stockings and it is still the chosen method for manufacturing them today.

As the popularity of knitted stockings grew, knitting rapidly became a domestic activity and an important source of income in many parts of rural England. The extra income from knitting stockings was an important part of the household budget.

The invention of a knitting frame around 1589 had little impact. Hand-knitted stockings remained in demand, and by the end of the 1600s, 200,000 English and Welsh knitters produced around 20 million pairs of stockings for the domestic market and 1.5 million pairs for export annually. This trade continued until the latter part of the eighteenth century.

There were several reasons for this. Hand knitting could be done almost anywhere and at any time and the hand knitter could respond instantly to changes in fashion. Hand knitters produced goods of varying types and quality that were sold at different prices. Another major factor was the importance of protecting the income from knitting for a large group of the populace. Fine hand-knitted stockings were thought to be superior in quality to those made by machine but they were also priced accordingly.

The Victorian Age

Anyone reading about the history of the needle arts could not fail to recognize the impact of the Victorian Age. The reign of Queen Victoria (1837–1901) saw a huge explosion in all sorts of handwork: embroidery, beadwork, and knitting all became fashionable pursuits for ladies.

New interest in knitting coincided with the development in trade with the wool growers of Saxony. Wool from this region was from merino sheep, a Spanish breed that produced silky, soft fleece that took dyes very well. Consequently, this fine wool, known as Berlin wool, was now available for knitting and needlepoint in beautiful colors. Victoria's husband, Albert, came from the center of this wool growing region and the Queen was a very prolific knitter until her death. This renewed interest in knitting led to the publication of numerous knitting "recipes," beginning around 1840. By 1847 this had turned into a flood of books of varying quality and price. They included instructions for a wide range of knitted items including baby clothes, shawls, caps, mittens, scarves, purses, and blankets. Some of these books were translated for sale in other parts of Europe and were reprinted in America.

Another important aspect of Victorian life was an increased awareness of life in other parts of the country and the world. The Great Exhibition of 1851 brought goods from around the world to the attention of the English as well as examples of domestic knitting and crochet. Victorian knitters were hungry for new inspiration and it often came in the form of traditional garments that were originally only made in isolated areas. Queen Victoria frequently wore a fine Shetland lace shawl knitted on the island of Unst, and this began a great fashion for such items. Fair Isle knitting, also from the Shetland Islands, and Argyle socks from Scotland became very popular as well.

At the same time that this new passion for hand knitting was sweeping across England, machine knitting was also developing and machine-made garments became more widely available.

Knitting for War

By the outbreak of the First World War in 1914, Victoria had died and the fashion for lavish decoration had been overtaken by the elegance of Art Nouveau. Knitting for this new war became an obsession. Vast quantities of socks, scarves, mittens, and helmets were sent to the soldiers in France. Knitting gave emotional comfort to the women who sat at home waiting for news from the front.

This passion for knitting continued once the war was over and public figures started trends in knitwear. In 1921 Edward VIII, who was then the Prince of Wales, wore a sleeveless Fair Isle vest while playing golf, beginning a craze for this style of knitting. Fashion designers like Coco Chanel and Elsa Shiaparelli saw the huge potential that knitted fabrics offered for fashion wear and quickly introduced knitted garments to their collections. Gone were the days when people dressed in voluminous folds of fabric, concealing the body under layers and layers of cloth. Knit fabric was prized for its ease of wear and the way that it fitted closely to the body but did not restrict movement in any way. Yarn could be spun from wool, cotton, silk, linen, and rayon, and by the start of the 1940s synthetic fibers like nylon began to have an impact on the textile industry.

Much of this development was interrupted by the Second World War, and again the knitters swung into action for the troops. Rationing was introduced and, as knitting wool was part of this scheme, unraveling and re-knitting became a normal task for knitters.

Into the Twenty-first Century

In the years that followed the end of the war, hand knitting continued as an economical and effective way of producing practical clothing in the home. But machine-made garments and new "easy-care" fibers had an undeniable allure for consumers, and before long, hand knitting lost appeal to many. Available yarn colors were dull and uninspiring, and many knitting patterns lacked any real innovation and had little appeal to those interested in fashion. This was to change, however, with the emergence in the mid-1970s of designers like Patricia Roberts, who designed knits with high fashion in mind and presented the patterns in the same manner as glossy fashion magazines. This attracted a whole new group of knitters who were knitting for fun rather than for practicality. Yarn companies responded by extending their colorways and experimenting with fiber blends.

Roberts, in turn, inspired one of the best-known contemporary designers of knitwear, Kaffe Fasset, an artist whose liberal use of color and pattern enthralled his followers. Much of the appeal of his designs was that they were mainly worked in stockinette stitch. These designs did not require a high level of knitting expertise but they did require patience! Much of Kaffe Fassett's inspiration came from ethnic textiles and artifacts, and his simply shaped garments were a canvas that he generously covered with intricate and sophisticated pattern in glorious color schemes. These designs used wonderful yarns that often combined fibers: wool, angora, mohair, silk, cotton, and linen. This was an exciting and inspiring time for knitters, new and old, and the potential of knitted fabric was considerably extended.

Changes in fashion in the late '80s and early '90s and the huge influx of cheap imported knitwear eventually led to another lull in interest for knitting. Knitting and other "domestic" skills fell out of favor in the education systems of most countries and the development of computer technology changed both work and leisure activities. The cost of buying yarn compared unfavorably to the cost of buying ready-made garments, and the movement of women to work outside the home meant that there was little time allocated for such pursuits.

The turn of a new century has seen a rekindled interest in knitting. Fun novelty yarns knitted into simple, easy-to-knit scarves have been the starting point for thousands of new knitters. There has also been an influx of exciting new fibers—yarns made from bamboo, soy, hemp, alpaca, camel, and microfiber, just to name a few.

There are hand-painted and hand-dyed yarns now available, pure cashmere and other exotic blends, felted yarns, self-striping sock wool, ribbon yarns; the list goes on and on. Beautiful needles made from bamboo, rosewood, and ebony make knitting a joy.

The emphasis is now on the quality of the yarn and the style and fit of the garment—a contrast to the unisex shapes that made knitting popular in the early 1980s.

Felted knitting, reminiscent of the caps of thirteenth-century England, has become enormously popular for making hats and bags. Many of these designs are fashionable and sophisticated. Sock knitting has had a new lease on life. Few people now knit for purely practical reasons, so knitting is not viewed as a chore or difficult task. Knitters take up their needles because they want to. They enjoy the relaxing, repetitive nature of knitting; the pleasure of creating something with their own hands; and the time away from busy, demanding jobs and a frantic lifestyle.

Before You Begin

Types of Yarn

Your choice of yarn will determine the overall look of the garment. A range of different fibers, both natural and synthetic, is used to create the fabulous selection of yarns that are available for today's knitter. Natural fibers are derived from either animals or plants. Different fibers are often blended together to create yarns that exhibit the best properties of their component fibers.

Natural animal fibers

Alpaca is a very fine, soft yarn that comes from the animal of the same name. Alpacas are related to llamas.

Angora is is made from the shorn fur of angora rabbits. It is very fine, lightweight, and has the ability to absorb considerable amounts of moisture before it feels wet.

Camel hair has a wonderful sheen. It does not accept dye, so it is often mixed with other fibers.

Cashmere is combed from the backs of cashmere goats. This silky, soft fiber is very expensive but also extremely warm.

Mohair is a hairy yarn obtained from angora goats. The yarn from very young goats is known as kid mohair. Mohair accepts dyes readily.

Silk is a luxurious fiber taken from the cocoons of silk worms. Comfortable to wear, it keeps you warm when the weather is cool and cool when the weather is warm.

Wool is often used as a generic term for knitting yarn, but it applies more specifically to the fleece of sheep. It accepts dyes easily and is particularly warm and durable. Lamb's wool is obtained from the very first shearing of an animal and is particularly soft. Shetland wool is a coarser wool taken from the backs of Shetland sheep. It is mainly used to create country tweed yarns.

Natural plant fibers

Cotton is an easy-care, cool-to-wear yarn, but it lacks the elasticity of wool.

Linen was one of the first fibers used by humans for making fabric. It makes a strong, stiff yarn. However, it is usually blended with other fibers to soften it.

Ramie is very similar in appearance and handling properties to linen. Like linen, it is usually combined with other fibers when making a knitting yarn.

Rayon is spun from cellulose and readily accepts dyes. It is not very resilient, so it can easily stretch out of shape.

Synthetic fibers

Most synthetic fibers are derived from coal or petroleum and they are generally inexpensive and easy to care for. On the down side, they will not withstand high temperatures and are very susceptible to static cling. Nylons, acrylics, and polyesters all fall into this category.

Jo Sharp
DK cotton

Patons Jet
(wool/alpaca)

Filatura di Crosa
Drifters (mohair/
acrylic)

Cleckheaton
Mousse 8 ply
(acrylic/wool/
viscose)

Cleckheaton
Deluxe Velvet
Ribbon (nylon/
acrylic)

Gedifra Sheela
(wool/acrylic/
nylon)

Textures

As well as knitting yarns being created from so many different fibers, there is also an extraordinary range of textures.

Double knitting yarn is a popular, smooth, even, hard-wearing yarn.

Bouclé yarn is made up of irregular loops twisted together. These are supported on a thinner straight thread.

Ribbon yarns are flat rather than rounded, just like ribbon. They are usually made of cotton or synthetic fibers.

Nubby yarns have small, irregularly placed pieces of yarn incorporated in them. They are often a different color to the rest of the yarn.

Chenille yarns are generally made from cotton or synthetic fibers. They create a soft, plush fabric.

Denim yarns actually fade with washing in the same way as denim jeans.

Mélange yarns have various colors that are mixed together before the yarn is spun.

Mouline yarns are created by twisting together either different colors of yarn or different types of fibers.

Hints

When beginning a project, always buy all the yarn you will need to complete it. Shades can vary from dye lot to dye lot.

When using a yarn different from the one recommended in the pattern, it is doubly important to knit a gauge swatch and check your needle size. Try to choose a yarn that is a similar weight to the original yarn.

Needles

There are three basic types of needles—the standard "pin" style, double-pointed, and circular. All of these come in a variety of diameters and lengths. Choose a diameter that suits the yarn you are using and the gauge you knit at. Most patterns will give a recommendation for the size of needle most suitable for knitting the yarn it specifies. Use this as your starting point and alter it according to your gauge swatch (see page 14).

Ensure your needles are long enough to hold the number of stitches you will be knitting. This is particularly important for circular needles, where the length should fit the number of required stitches without stretching them out too much. Shorter needles are generally easier to use but you do not want to have to squeeze stitches onto your needles. They have a habit of slipping off when you are not looking!

Double-pointed needles for knitting in the round usually come in sets of four. Cable needles are also pointed at both ends. These can be perfectly straight or they can have a kink in the middle. The kink will make the needle less likely to slip out of position at the wrong time, but it is really a matter of personal preference.

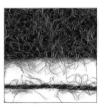

Yarn Bee
Highland Thistle
(acrylic)

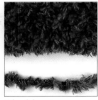

Cleckheaton
Fab Fur
(wool/acrylic)

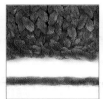

Sirdar Wow
(polyester)

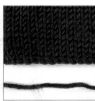

Cleckheaton
Merino (wool)

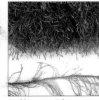

Sullivans Plumes
(polyester)

Filatura Di Crosa
Sympathie
(mohair/wool/
acrylic)

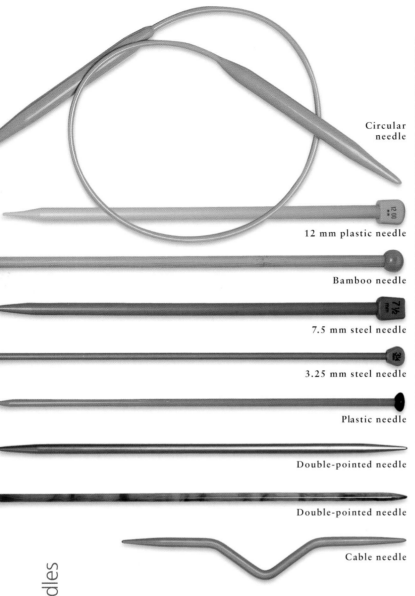

Circular needle

12 mm plastic needle

Bamboo needle

7.5 mm steel needle

3.25 mm steel needle

Plastic needle

Double-pointed needle

Double-pointed needle

Cable needle

Sizes - conversion chart

Metric sizes	US sizes	Old UK & Canadian sizes
1 mm	-	20
1.25 mm	-	18
1.5 mm	-	16
1.75 mm	-	15
2 mm	0	14
2.25 mm	1	13
2.5 mm	-	-
2.75 mm	2	12
3 mm	-	11
3.25 mm	3	10
3.5 mm	4	-
3.75 mm	5	9
4 mm	6	8
4.5 mm	7	7
5 mm	8	6
5.5 mm	9	5
6 mm	10	4
6.5 mm	10½	3
7 mm	10¾	2
7.5 mm	-	1
8 mm	11	0
9 mm	13	00
10 mm	15	000

Needles can be made from a variety of materials. Plastic, bamboo, and aluminium are the most common, but you do still find steel and beautiful wooden needles.

Needles are made to conform to a standard sizing system. The only problem is that there are three standard sizing systems that are widely used throughout the world—a metric system, an American system, and an old English and Canadian system.

Other Tools and Equipment

As well as standard items such as scissors, pins, tape measures, and rulers, there are numerous specialty items that will make your knitting more pleasurable.

Row counters

Row counters

These clever devices allow you to keep a count of the rows you have worked. This is particularly useful when stitching a design where several rows are required for each pattern repeat or when matching a front to a back. The trick is remembering to advance the number after each row is completed.

Stitch holders

Stitch holders do exactly what their name suggests. They hold a group of stitches that you need to set aside for working on later, such as for neck shapings, pocket bands, or shoulder seams that will be grafted together. Many of them look like large safety pins. In fact, a safety pin can be used for holding a small number of stitches. A length of contrast yarn makes a great stitch holder for stitches that are around a curve.

Yarn bobbins

Yarn bobbins help you manage your yarn when you are knitting with multiple colors such as for intarsia knitting (see page 100). There are several shapes and sizes available. Experiment and select the ones you find easiest to use. You can also make your own bobbins by cutting pieces from cardboard or template plastic.

Crochet hooks

Crochet hooks are excellent for picking up dropped stitches and can also be used for binding off. Like knitting needles, they are available in a range of sizes, so choose one that suits the weight of the yarn you are using.

Needle gauge

A needle gauge allows you to check the size of a particular set of needles. This is very useful for double-pointed needles, which don't have the size marked on them, and when using a pattern that lists needle sizes in a different sizing system to your needles. Most gauges provide conversions to at least one other sizing system.

Point protectors

These little items slip onto the tips of your needles when you are not knitting. They ensure that your stitches stay put while you are not there.

Stitch and row markers

These are particularly useful when knitting in the round so that you can easily determine where a new row starts, or for identifying different sections of a pattern such as the beginning of armhole shaping. Commercially made markers come in a variety of shapes and colors. A short length or loop of contrast yarn can also be used as a stitch or row marker.

Sewing needles

Use a needle with a large eye and blunt tip so that you do not split your knitting stitches. Tapestry needles are the perfect choice and they come in sizes ranging from 18 to 28. Darning needles are longer than tapestry needles and are also an excellent choice.

Baskets, bags, and boxes

These are useful for keeping your yarn under control and for keeping all the components of your project together—particularly if you have a furry member in your family that finds those balls of yarn oh, so tempting.

Gauge

This is the key to having your knitted pieces turn out the correct size. Everyone's knitting gauge is a little different and, of course, this little difference is multiplied by every stitch you make.

Gauge is affected by the way you hold the yarn and needles, the type of yarn you are using, the size of the needles, and the pattern of the stitches.

Hints

Depending on your stitch pattern, you may find it easier to count the rows on the back of the knitted fabric.

If your yarn is particularly fluffy or hairy, place your swatch on a lightbox or against a window to make it easier to count the rows and stitches.

If your gauge swatch is made of ribbing, slightly stretch it sideways before measuring.

How to measure gauge

Most patterns provide instructions for measuring gauge.

Using your planned yarn, needles, and stitch pattern (or the stitch pattern indicated by the garment pattern), work a swatch that is at least 5" (12.5 cm) square. Measure 4" (10 cm) across the middle of the swatch and mark with pins. Count the number of stitches between the two pins. Repeat this process vertically, counting the number of rows. Compare your findings with those in the pattern.

Altering gauge

If you have more rows or stitches within the 4" (10 cm) area than the pattern indicated, it means your tension is too firm. Change to a larger set of needles and knit another swatch.

If you have fewer rows or stitches within the 4" (10 cm) area than the pattern indicated, it means your tension is too loose. Change to a smaller set of needles and knit another swatch.

While this may seem tedious, it is well worth taking the time to achieve the right gauge before beginning your garment.

8-ply cotton yarn
knitted with 3.25 mm needles

8-ply cotton yarn
knitted with 4.25 mm needles

8-ply cotton yarn
knitted with 6 mm needles

Abbreviations

alt	alternate
beg	begin(ning)
CC	contrasting color
cm	centimeter(s)
cont	continue(ing)(s)
cr	cross
C4L	cable of 4 stitches to the left
C4R	cable of 4 stitches to the right
dec	decrease(ing)(s)
DK	double knitting
dpn(s)	double-pointed needle(s)
foll	following
inc	increase(ing)(s)
incl	including
K	knit
K1b&f	knit into the back and then the front of the same stitch
K1f&b	knit into the front and then the back of the same stitch
K2tog	knit 2 together
K3tog	knit 3 together
LH	left hand
LT	left twist
MB	make a bobble
MC	main color
M1	make 1
M1 tbl	make 1 through the back of the loop
mm	millimeter(s)
oz	ounce(s)
P	purl
patt	pattern(s)
P1b&f	purl into the back and then the front of the same stitch
P1f&b	purl into the front and then the back of the same stitch
pnso	pass next stitch over
psso	pass the slipped stitch over
p2sso	pass 2 slipped stitches over
P2tog	purl 2 together
rem	remain(ing)
rep(s)	repeat(s)
rev St st	reverse stockinette stitch(es)
RH	right hand
rnd(s)	round(s)
RS	right side
RT	right twist
sk	skip
skpo	slip 1, knit 1, pass the slipped stitch over
sl	slip
sl st(s)	slip stitch(es)
ssk	slip, slip knit
st(s)	stitch(es)
St st(s)	stockinette stitch(es)
tbl	through back of loop(s)
tog	together
WS	wrong side
wyib	with yarn in back
wyif	with yarn in front
yb	take the yarn to the back between the 2 needles
yd(s)	yard(s)
yfwd	bring the yarn to the front between the 2 needles
YO(s)	yarn over(s)

Symbols

On a chart, every square represents one stitch and one row of squares equals one row of knitting. The odd-numbered rows are the right-side rows and the even-numbered rows are the wrong-side rows.

Commonly used symbols

cable of 4 stitches to the left	
cable of 4 stitches to the right	
knit 2 together on a right-side row or purl 2 together on a wrong-side row	
left twist	
make a bobble	
make 1	
make 1 through back of loop	
purl 2 together on a right-side row or knit 2 together on a wrong-side row	
reverse stockinette stitch	
right twist	
selvage stitch	
stockinette stitch	
yarn over	

patterns and charts before you begin

Basic Stitches and Techniques

There are two basic ways to knit—the Continental method and the English method. The method you choose will affect the way you hold the yarn and needles. In the Continental method of knitting, the yarn is held with your left hand. The English method requires you to hold the yarn with your right hand.

Experiment with the various ways and choose one that suits you. You want to be able to feed the yarn smoothly and easily around the needle while maintaining some tension on it. It is the job of your index finger to place the yarn around the needle and the job of your three remaining fingers to provide the tension.

Except for casting on, binding off, and essential stitches, the instructions in this book are written for the English method.

Holding the Yarn and Needles
Left-Handed Yarn Holds

Method 1

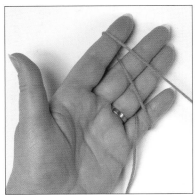 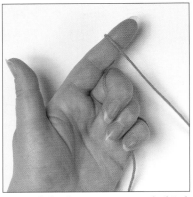

1. Wrap the yarn clockwise around your little finger. Carry it across the front of your third and second finger. Take it behind and over your index finger between your first and second knuckle.

2. Lightly close your second, third, and little fingers around the yarn.

Method 2

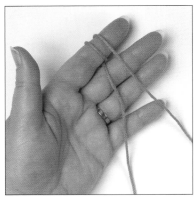 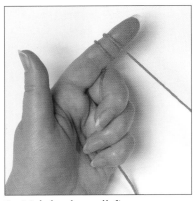

1. Take the yarn across the front of your little, third, and second fingers. Wrap the yarn clockwise around your index finger one-and-a-half times. Ensure the wraps lie between your first and second knuckles.

2. Lightly close all fingers, except your index finger, around the yarn.

Right-Handed Yarn Holds

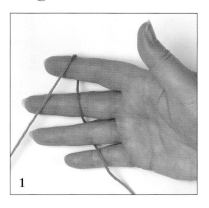

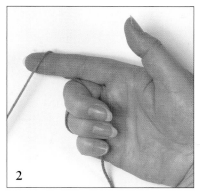

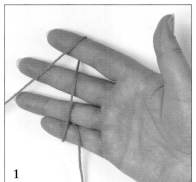

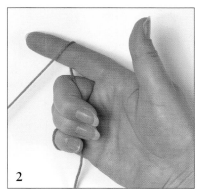

Method 1

1. Weave the yarn under your little finger, over your third finger, under your second finger, and then over your index finger. Keep it between your index finger's nail and first knuckle.

2. Lightly close your second, third, and little fingers around the yarn.

Method 2

1. Wrap the yarn counterclockwise around your little finger. Carry it across the front of your third and second finger. Take it behind and over your index finger between the first and second knuckle.

2. Lightly close your second, third and little fingers around the yarn.

Needle Holds

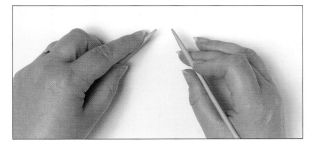

Method 1

This method is particularly suitable when using longer needles because the end of your right needle can be tucked into your armpit for additional support.

Hold both needles as you would hold a knife with your thumb resting on the side approximately 1" (2.5 cm) from the tip of the needle, your index finger resting on top, and your three remaining fingers providing support.

Method 2

This method works best with short needles.

Hold your left needle in the same manner as in method 1 and hold your right needle as you would hold a pencil, supporting it in the crook of your thumb and index finger.

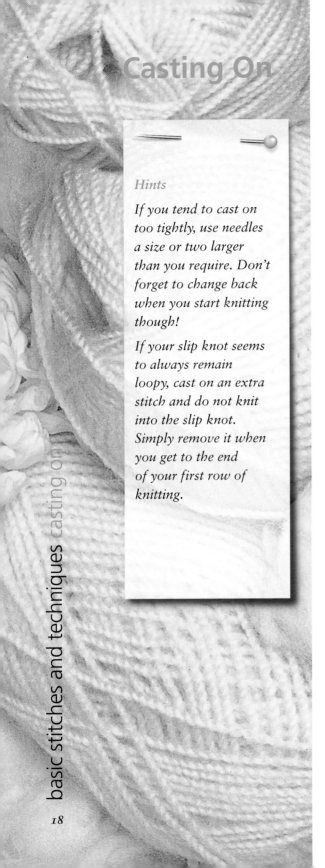

Hints

If you tend to cast on too tightly, use needles a size or two larger than you require. Don't forget to change back when you start knitting though!

If your slip knot seems to always remain loopy, cast on an extra stitch and do not knit into the slip knot. Simply remove it when you get to the end of your first row of knitting.

Slip Knot

All casting on techniques begin with a slip knot.

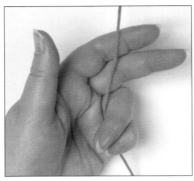

1. Hold the end of the yarn across the palm of your hand with your third and little fingers.

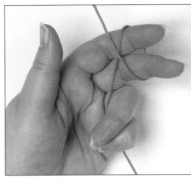

2. Wrap the yarn around your index and second fingers, wrapping twice in a clockwise direction.

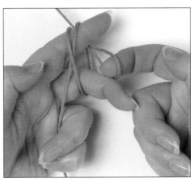

3. Spread your index and second fingers and take the yarn between your fingers and through the loop. A new loop will form.

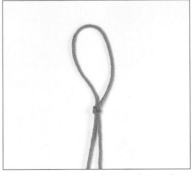

4. Pull the loop of yarn through to tighten the knot.

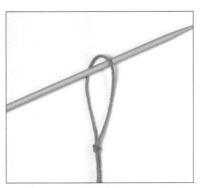

5. Place this new loop onto your needle.

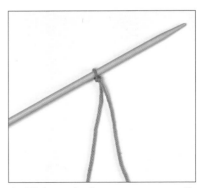

6. Tighten the loop on your needle by pulling on the ball end of the yarn.

basic stitches and techniques casting on

Cable Cast On This method creates quite a firm, hard-wearing edge.

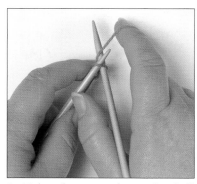

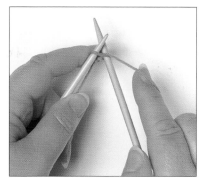

1. With the slip knot on your left needle, insert the tip of your right needle from left to right through the loop. Take it behind your left needle.

2. Take the yarn from the ball around the tip of your right needle from the back to the front.

3. Pull the yarn downward between your two needles until it rests on the loop.

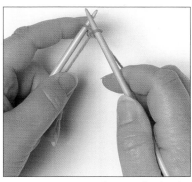

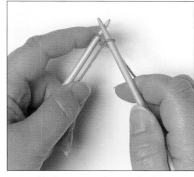

4. Draw your right needle backward so that the slip knot glides to the tip of your needle. As you reach the tip, twist it to pick up the yarn between your needles.

5. Pull the yarn through, forming a loop on your right needle.

Hints

Taking your needle from left to right through the loop on your right needle (see step 6) will create the same result. You just need to be consistent with the way you choose.

Do not tighten the stitches on your left needle too much or you will find it difficult to work the first row of knitting.

Leave a tail of at least 4" (10 cm) and use this for sewing up the seam.

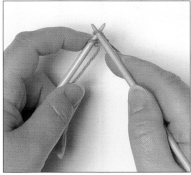

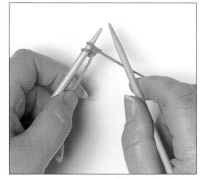

6. Take your left needle from right to left through the loop on your right needle.

7. Remove your right needle from the loop. There are now two loops (or stitches) on your left needle.

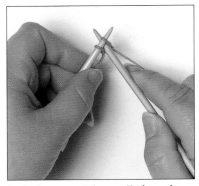

8. Take your right needle from front to back between the two stitches. Pull yarn from the ball to tighten.

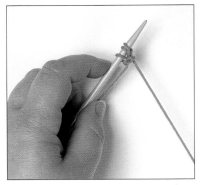

9. Repeat steps 2–8 to complete the third stitch.

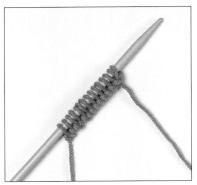

10. Continue working the required number of stitches in the same manner.

Cable cast on

English thumb cast on

Continental thumb cast on

Thumb Cast On:
English Style

This method creates an edge with more elasticity than cable cast on.

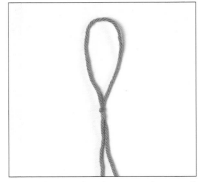

1. Make a slip knot with a tail long enough to work the required number of cast-on stitches.

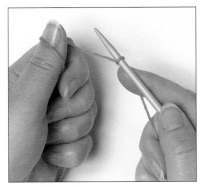

2. Hold your needle with the slip knot as well as the yarn to the ball with your right hand (see page 17). Take the tail of yarn from back to front around your left thumb and hold it with your fingers.

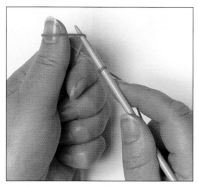

3. Take your needle from bottom to top through the loop of yarn around your left thumb.

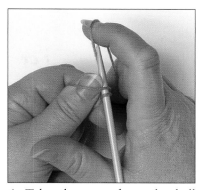

4. Take the yarn from the ball from back to front around the tip of your needle in a counterclockwise direction.

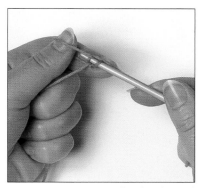

5. Draw your needle backward through the loop on your thumb.

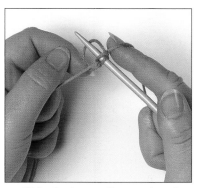

6. Slide the loop off your thumb.

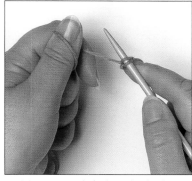

7. Twist your left thumb clockwise to pick up a second loop of yarn. At the same time, pull the yarn to tighten the new loop on your needle.

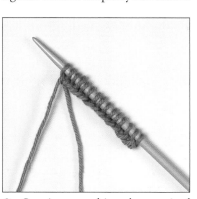

8. Repeat steps 3–7 to complete a third stitch.

9. Continue working the required number of stitches in the same manner.

Hints

As a guide, 39" (1 m) of yarn will create approximately 100 stitches. This will vary with the thickness of yarn and your gauge. It is better to make the tail longer than you think you will need. The excess can be used later for sewing seams.

If you require a particularly loose edge, cast on over two needles held together. Remove one needle before you begin knitting.

casting on basic stitches and techniques

Thumb Cast On: Continental Style

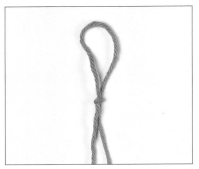

1. Make a slip knot with a tail long enough to work the required number of cast-on stitches.

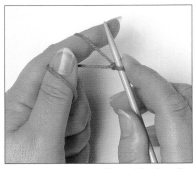

2. Hold your needle with the slip knot in your right hand. Hold the tail end of the yarn in the same way as the English method. Take the ball end of the yarn over your left index finger and hold it with the tail end.

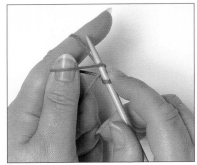

3. Take your needle from bottom to top through the loop of yarn around your left thumb.

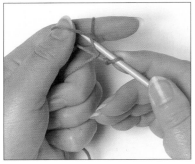

4. Take your needle from right to left behind the yarn over your index finger.

5. Take your needle back through the loop of yarn around your left thumb.

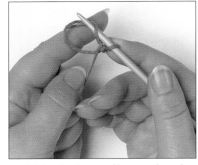

6. Slide the loop off your thumb.

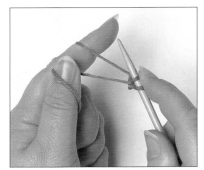

7. Twist your left thumb clockwise to pick up a second loop of yarn. At the same time, pull both ends of the yarn to tighten the new loop on your needle.

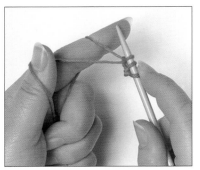

8. Repeat steps 3–7 to complete a third stitch.

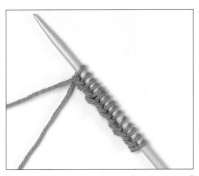

9. Continue working the required number of stitches in the same manner.

Tubular Cast On

This method is also known as invisible cast on and creates a hard-wearing edge that can be used for single ribbing.

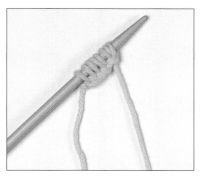

1. Using a contrasting yarn and the cable cast-on method, cast on half the required number of stitches. If necessary, add an extra stitch to ensure you have an even number.

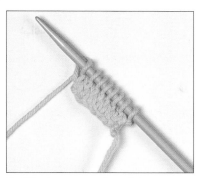

2. Work a row of purl (see pages 28–29) and then a row of knit (see pages 26–27).

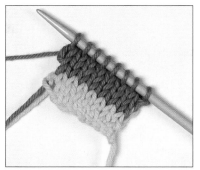

3. Join in the main yarn. Beginning with a row of purl, work four rows of stockinette stitch (see page 30).

4. Purl the first stitch of the next row.

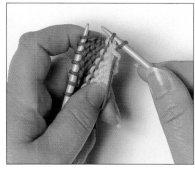

5. Take the yarn between your needles to the back. Take your right needle from top to bottom behind the first loop of the first row worked with the main yarn.

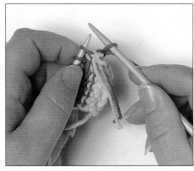

6. Transfer the loop to your left needle.

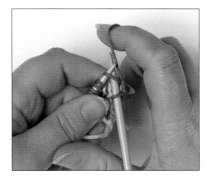

7. Work a knit stitch into this new loop.

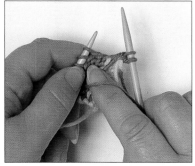

8. Bring the yarn to the front between your two needles.

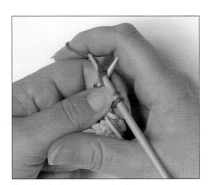

9. Purl the next stitch.

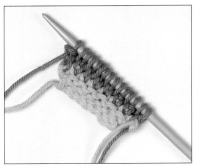

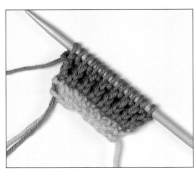

10. Repeat steps 5–9 across the row. You will end up with twice the number of stitches, less one.

11. Work knit one, purl one across the next row.

12. Continue working the desired number of rows with the single rib pattern.

13. Pull the loose end of the contrast yarn firmly, gathering the stitches.

14. Cut the yarn close to the stitching. Smooth out the knitting and the first few stitches will separate from the main section.

15. Repeat steps 13–14 until the contrast yarn is completely removed.

Guernsey Cast On This makes a decorative edge traditionally used for Guernsey sweaters.

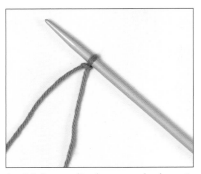

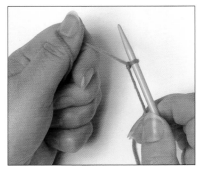

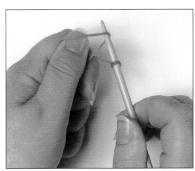

1. Make a slip knot and place it on your right needle.

2. Hold the needle with the slip knot in your right hand. Take the yarn from the ball from back to front around your left thumb and hold it with your fingers.

3. Take your needle from bottom to top through the loop of yarn around your left thumb.

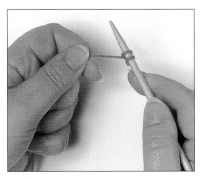

4. Slip the loop onto your needle and tighten.

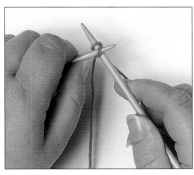

5. Using a second needle, pick up the slip knot.

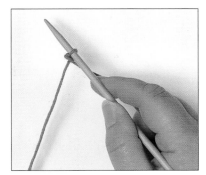

6. Pass the slip knot over the cast-on stitch and take it off your needles.

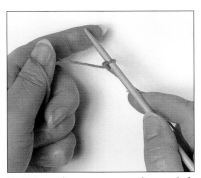

7. Wrap the yarn around your left thumb as before.

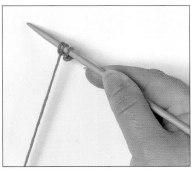

8. Add two more cast-on stitches following steps 3–4.

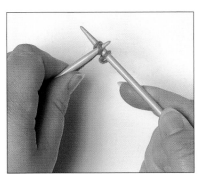

9. Using a second needle, pick up the first of the two cast-on stitches you just worked.

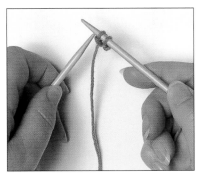

10. Pass the stitch over the last cast-on stitch and off your needle.

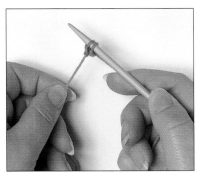

11. Pull the yarn from the ball to tighten the stitch.

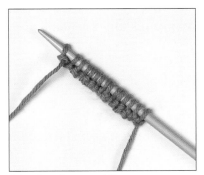

12. Continue adding two cast-on stitches and slipping the first stitch over the second stitch as before until the required number of stitches are worked.

casting on basic stitches and techniques

25

The Essential Stitches: Knit and Purl

Knit and purl stitch form the basis of almost every knitted fabric.

Knit Stitch: English Style

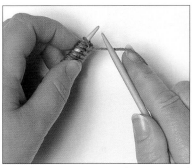

1. After casting on the required number of stitches, hold the needle with the stitches in your left hand. Hold empty needle and yarn with your right hand (see pages 16–17).

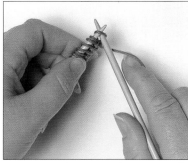

2. Insert the tip of your right needle from left to right into the front of the first stitch. The tip of your needle will end up behind your left needle.

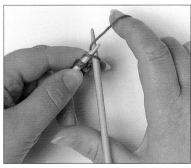

3. Wrap the yarn from back to front between the tips of your two needles.

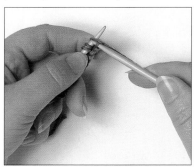

4. Draw the tip of your right needle back through the stitch on your left needle. Keep the wrapped yarn on your right needle.

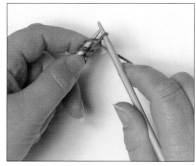

5. The wrapped yarn will form a new stitch on your right needle.

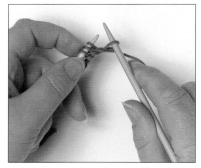

6. Slide your right needle to the right, slipping the used loop on the tip of your left needle off the needle.

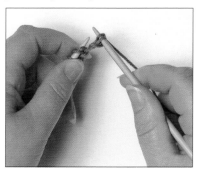

7. Repeat steps 2–6 to form a second stitch.

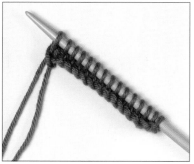

8. Continue to the end of the row in the same manner.

Hint

Always keep the yarn behind your needles for knit stitch and in front of them for purl stitch.

basic stitches and techniques the essential stitches

26

Knit Stitch: Continental Style

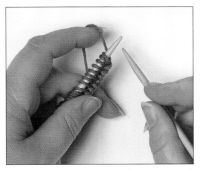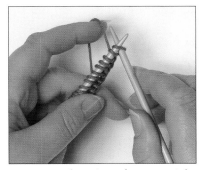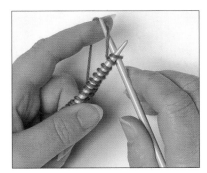

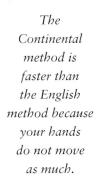

The Continental method is faster than the English method because your hands do not move as much.

1. After casting on the required number of stitches, hold the yarn and the needle with the stitches in your left hand. Hold your empty needle with your right hand (see pages 16–17).

2. Insert the tip of your right needle from left to right into the front of the first stitch. The tip of your needle will end up behind your left needle.

3. Twist your right needle so that it passes from right to left behind the yarn coming from your left index finger.

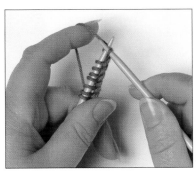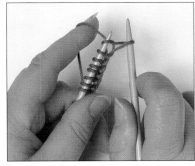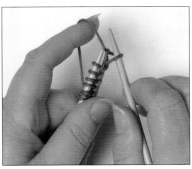

4. Slide your right needle back through the stitch on your left needle, taking the picked up loop of yarn with it.

5. The yarn will form a new stitch on your right needle.

6. Slip the used loop on the tip of your left needle off the needle.

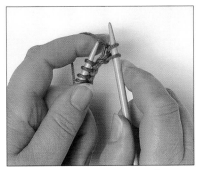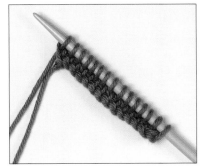

7. Repeat steps 2–6 to form a second stitch.

8. Continue to the end of the row in the same manner.

Hint

When you have knitted all the stitches across a row, all your stitches will be on your right needle. Swap the needles over so that all the stitches are on the needle you hold in your left hand. Stitch across the row as before. Keep swapping the needles over after each row.

the essential stitches · basic stitches and techniques

27

Purl Stitch: English Style

Purl stitch is really just the opposite of knit stitch. It can be trickier to work using the Continental method than the English method.

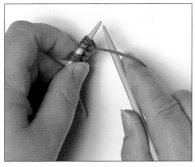

1. After casting on the required number of stitches, hold the needle with the stitches in your left hand. Hold the empty needle and yarn with your right hand (see pages 16–17).

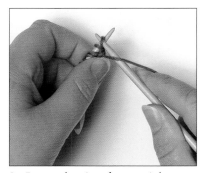

2. Insert the tip of your right needle from right to left into the front of the first stitch. Both the yarn and the tip of your right needle will end up in front of your left needle.

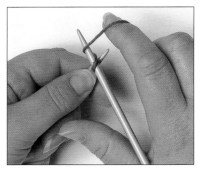

3. Wrap the yarn from right to left (counterclockwise) around the tip of your right needle.

4. Keeping tension on the yarn, slide your right needle back until the tip is against your left needle.

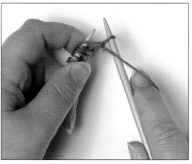

5. Take the tip of your right needle back through the loop on your left needle, keeping the wrapped yarn on your right needle. The wrapped yarn will form a new stitch on your right needle.

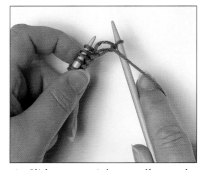

6. Slide your right needle to the right, slipping the used loop on the tip of your left needle off the needle.

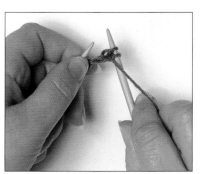

7. Repeat steps 2–6 to form a second stitch.

8. Continue to the end of the row in the same manner.

Hint

The first row of knitting is always the hardest to knit because your tension hasn't been fully established.

Purl Stitch: Continental Style

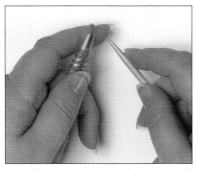

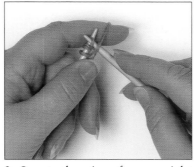

When working purl stitch with the Continental method, begin and end each row with a knit stitch to create a firmer edge.

1. After casting on the required number of stitches, hold the yarn and the needle with the stitches in your left hand. Hold your empty needle with your right hand (see pages 16–17).

2. Insert the tip of your right needle from right to left behind the yarn and into the front of the first stitch. Both the yarn and the tip of your right needle are in front of your left needle.

3. Tilt your right needle to an upright position. Wrap the yarn from right to left (counterclockwise) around the tip of your right needle.

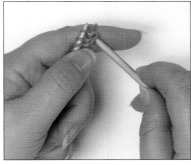

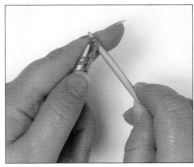

4. Holding the yarn downward behind the stitch, slide your right needle back until the tip is against your left needle.

5. Take the tip of your right needle back through the loop on your left needle, keeping the wrapped yarn on your right needle. The wrapped yarn will form a new stitch on your right needle.

6. Slide your right needle to the left, slipping the used loop on the tip of your left needle off the needle.

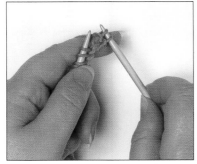

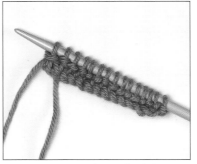

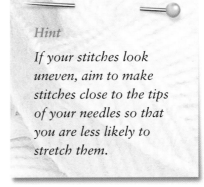

Hint

If your stitches look uneven, aim to make stitches close to the tips of your needles so that you are less likely to stretch them.

7. Repeat steps 2–6 to form a second stitch.

8. Continue to the end of the row in the same manner.

the essential stitches basic stitches and techniques

29

Other Basic Stitches

Garter stitch

After casting on the required number of stitches, work every row with knit stitch. Both sides of the knitted fabric look the same.

Stockinette stitch

Stockinette stitch is also known as stocking stitch. After casting on the required number of stitches, work the first row with knit stitch and then the second row with purl stitch. Alternate rows of knit and purl stitch.

Reverse stockinette stitch

This stitch looks the same as the reverse side of stockinette stitch. After casting on the required number of stitches, work the first row with purl stitch and then the second row with knit stitch. Alternate rows of purl and knit stitch.

Moss stitch

Moss stitch is also known as seed stitch.

Cast on an even number of stitches. Knit one, purl one alternately across the first row. Purl one, knit one alternately across the second row. Repeat these two rows.

Binding Off
Binding off allows you to remove your needles without having all your precious knitting unravel before your eyes.

Binding Off in Knit Stitch

1. Hold the needle with the stitches in your left hand. Knit the first two stitches.

2. Insert the tip of your left needle from left to right into the front of the first stitch on your right needle.

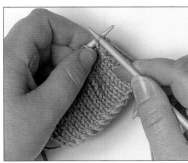

3. Take the stitch over the second stitch and off your right needle.

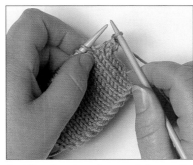

4. Slip the tip of your left needle out of the stitch so that it drops below the one stitch remaining on your right needle.

5. Knit the next stitch on your left needle.

6. Repeat steps 2–4 to cast off the next stitch.

7. Continue until there are no stitches on your left needle and one stitch on your right needle. Cut yarn, leaving a 4" (10 cm) tail. Loosen the loop and remove the needle. Thread the tail through the loop.

8. Pull the tail firmly to tighten the loop.

Binding Off in Purl Stitch

1. Hold the needle with the stitches in your left hand. Purl the first two stitches.

2. Insert the tip of your left needle from left to right into the front of the first stitch on your right needle.

3. Take the stitch over the second stitch and off your right needle.

4. Slip the tip of your left needle out of the stitch so that it drops below the one stitch remaining on your right needle.

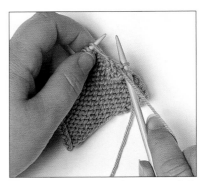

5. Purl the next stitch on your left needle.

6. Repeat steps 2–4 to cast off the next stitch.

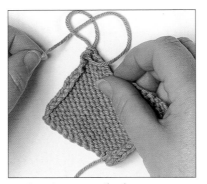

7. Continue until there are no stitches on your left needle and one stitch on your right needle. Cut the yarn, leaving a tail at least 4" (10 cm) long. Loosen the loop on your needle and remove the needle. Thread the tail through the loop.

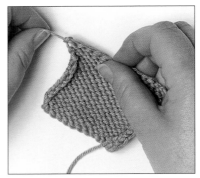

8. Pull the tail firmly to tighten the loop.

Binding Off by Knitting Stitches Together

This method creates a firm edge with very little stretch. It is particularly suitable for finishing off shoulder seams and cable patterns. It can also be worked using purl instead of knit stitch, or following the pattern of your knitted fabric.

Hints

A bound-off edge should have the same elasticity as the knitted fabric you have just created.

Always bind off using the same stitches as if you were knitting the row following your pattern.

If you have a tendency to bind off too tightly, change to a larger needle.

After binding off, leave a tail of yarn long enough to sew up the seam.

1. Hold the needle with the stitches in your left hand. Insert your right needle from left to right into the first two stitches on your left needle.

2. Knit as for one stitch, passing both loops off your left needle. One stitch remains on your right needle.

3. Insert the tip of your left needle from the back to the front of the stitch on your right needle.

4. Remove your right needle from the stitch, leaving it on your left needle.

5. Knit the first two stitches on your left needle together in the same manner as before.

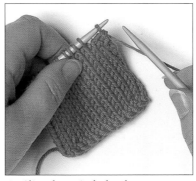

6. Slip the stitch back onto your left needle following steps 3–4.

7. Continue until only one stitch remains. Cut the yarn, leaving a 4" (10 cm) tail. Loosen the loop on your needle and remove the needle. Thread the tail through the loop.

8. Pull the tail firmly to tighten the loop.

Using knit stitch

Using purl stitch

Binding Off Two Edges Together

This method, also known as three-needle bind off, joins two pieces together with an invisible join. Both pieces must have exactly the same number of stitches.

1. Hold the two needles with the stitches on in your left hand. The right sides of the knitted fabric face each other. Cut yarn from front piece, leaving a 4" (10 cm) tail.

2. Using a third needle in your right hand, take the tip through the back of the first stitch on your front needle and through the front of the first stitch on your back needle.

3. Hold the two left needles close together. Using the yarn from the back piece, wrap it from back to front between your left and right needles.

4. Slide the two stitches over the yarn and off your left needle, forming a knit stitch.

basic stitches and techniques binding off

5. Repeat steps 2–4 to form a second stitch.

6. Insert the tip of your back left needle from left to right into the front of the first stitch on your right needle.

7. Take this stitch over the second stitch and off your right needle.

8. Work another stitch following steps 2–4.

9. Slip the first stitch on your right needle over the newest stitch in the same manner as before.

10. Continue in the same manner until your left needles are empty and only one stitch remains on your right needle.

11. Cut the yarn, leaving a tail at least 4" (10 cm) long. Loosen the loop on your needle and remove the needle. Thread the tail through the loop.

12. Pull the tail firmly to tighten the loop.

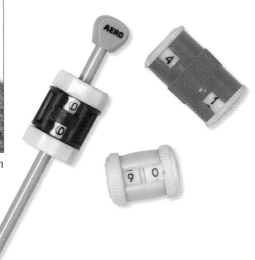

binding off basic stitches and techniques

35

Joining In a New Yarn

Wherever possible, join in a new yarn at the beginning of a row. It can be difficult to hide a join and the tails of yarn in the middle of a row.

Joining In a New Yarn at the Beginning of a Row

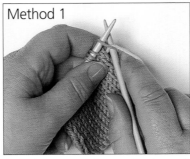

Method 1

1. Take your right needle through the first stitch on your left needle. Leaving a tail of yarn at least 4"(10 cm) long, loop the new yarn around your right needle.

2. Using the new yarn, work approximately six stitches.

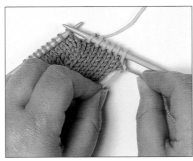

3. Tie the two tails of yarn together at the beginning of the row with a single knot.

4. After the piece is finished, undo the knot and finish off the tails of yarn by weaving them into a seam or the back of the knitting (see page 138).

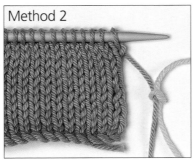

Method 2

1. Leaving a tail of yarn at least 4" (10 cm) long, tie a new yarn around the old yarn with a single knot.

2. Push the knot along the old yarn until it is close to the first stitch.

3. Stitch using the new yarn.

4. When finished, undo the knot and finish off the tails of yarn by weaving them into a seam or the back of the knitting (see page 138).

Joining In a New Yarn in the Middle of a Row

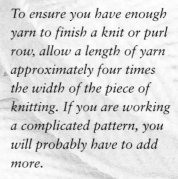

1. Take your right needle through the next stitch on your left needle. Leaving a tail of yarn at least 4" (10 cm) long, loop the new yarn around your right needle.

Hints

To ensure you have enough yarn to finish a knit or purl row, allow a length of yarn approximately four times the width of the piece of knitting. If you are working a complicated pattern, you will probably have to add more.

Always pull enough yarn from the ball to complete a row before you begin the row. This way you can check if there are any knots that are likely to appear in unwanted places.

If you need to join in a new yarn in the middle of a row, try and place the join as invisibly as possible, for example, at the edge of a cable.

2. Using the new yarn, work to the end of the row.

3. Loosely tie the two tails of yarn together.

4. When finished, undo the knot and finish off the tails of yarn by weaving them into the back of the knitting (see pages 138–139).

joining in a new yarn basic stitches and techniques

37

Selvages

Selvages are often unnecessary but some patterns will include instructions for a selvage.

Chain Stitch Selvage

This method forms a neat edge to garter stitch and is suitable for an exposed edge. You do need to be careful that you do not let the edge stitches become too loose.

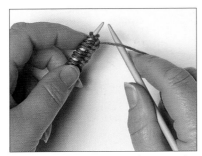

1. With the yarn in front, take your right needle from right to left through the front of the first stitch on your left needle, just like working a purl stitch.

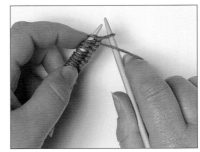

2. Slip the stitch off your left needle and onto your right needle.

3. Take the yarn to the back between the two needles.

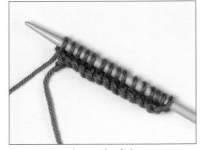

4. Knit to the end of the row.

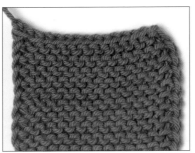

5. Repeat steps 1–4 for every row.

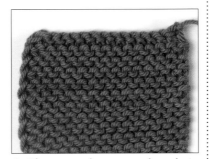

6. If you only want the chain stitches along one edge, alternate between stitching steps 1–4 and knitting across the entire row.

No Selvage

When working patterned knitting or edges that will be sewn together with back stitch, selvages are unnecessary.

Garter Stitch Selvage

The first and last stitch of every row is worked with knit stitch. This creates a firmer edge and the small ridges that form are excellent guides when using ladder stitch for sewing seams.

Shaping

Increasing and decreasing is used to shape a garment by adding or removing one to two stitches at a time. Work the increases or decreases when the right side of the knitted fabric is facing you.

Increasing: Bar Increase While Working Knit Stitch

This method creates a small horizontal bar, which can add a decorative touch and is also known as knitting twice into the same stitch.

1. At the position for the increase, take your right needle from left to right through the front of the first stitch on your left needle. The tip of your right needle will end up behind your left needle.

2. Wrap the yarn from back to front between the tips of your two needles.

3. Draw the tip of your right needle back through the stitch on your left needle. Keep the wrapped yarn on your right needle where it will form a new stitch.

4. Take the tip of your right needle from right to left through the back of the first stitch on your left needle. Again, the tip of your right needle will end up behind your left needle.

5. Wrap the yarn from back to front between the tips of your two needles.

6. Draw the tip of your right needle back through the stitch on your left needle. Keep the wrapped yarn on your right needle where it will form a new stitch.

7. Slide your right needle to the right, slipping off the used loop on the tip of your left needle. You now have two stitches for the price of one!

Increasing:
Bar Increase While Working Purl Stitch

A small horizontal bar is visible on the knit side of your fabric.

1. At the position for the increase, take your right needle from right to left through the front of the first stitch on your left needle. The tip of your right needle will end up in front of your left needle.

2. Wrap the yarn from right to left (counterclockwise) around the tip of your right needle.

3. Draw the tip of your right needle back through the stitch on your left needle. Keep the wrapped yarn on your right needle where it will form a new stitch.

4. Take the tip of your right needle from left to right through the back of the first stitch on your left needle. Finish with the tip of your right needle in front of your left needle and to the right of the front of the stitch.

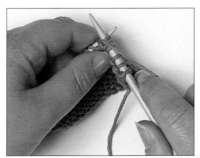

5. Wrap the yarn from right to left (counterclockwise) around the tip of your right needle.

6. Draw the tip of your right needle back through the stitch on your left needle. Keep the wrapped yarn on your right needle where it will form a new stitch.

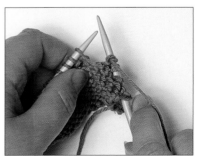

7. Slide your right needle to the right, slipping off the used loop on the tip of your left needle.

basic stitches and techniques shaping

40

Increasing:
Make One
on Knit Row

This method cannot be used on the very edge of the knitted fabric.

1. Knit to the position for the increase. Take your right needle from front to back under the yarn that lies between the stitch you just worked and the next stitch on your left needle.

2. Take the tip of your left needle from right to left under the front of this loop of yarn.

3. Slip the loop onto your left needle.

4. Take the tip of your right needle from right to left through the back of the loop on your left needle. The tip of your right needle will end up behind your left needle.

5. Wrap the yarn from back to front between the tips of your two needles.

6. Draw the tip of your right needle back through the stitch on your left needle. Keep the wrapped yarn on your right needle where it will form a new stitch.

7. Slide your right needle to the right, slipping off the used loop on the tip of your left needle. An extra stitch is now in position on your right needle.

Increasing: Make One on Purl Row

This method cannot be used on the very edge of the knitted fabric.

1. Purl to the position for the increase. Take your right needle from front to back under the yarn that lies between the stitch you just worked and the next stitch on your left needle.

2. Take the tip of your left needle from right to left under the front of this loop of yarn.

3. Slip the loop onto your left needle.

4. Take the tip of your right needle from left to right through the back of the loop on your left needle. Finish with the tip of your right needle in front of your left needle and to the right of the front of the stitch.

5. Wrap the yarn from right to left (counterclockwise) around the tip of your right needle.

6. Draw the tip of your right needle back through the stitch on your left needle. Keep the wrapped yarn on your right needle where it will form a new stitch.

7. Slide your right needle to the right, slipping off the used loop on the tip of your left needle.

Increasing: Yarn Over While Working Knit Stitch

This method will create a hole in the knitted fabric.

1. Knit to the position for the increase. Bring the yarn forward between the two needles.

2. Insert the tip of your right needle from left to right into the first stitch on your left needle as you would for a knit stitch.

3. Beginning and ending with the yarn at the front, wrap it from right to left (counterclockwise) around the tip of your right needle.

4. Draw the tip of your right needle back through the stitch on your left needle. Keep the wrapped yarn on your right needle.

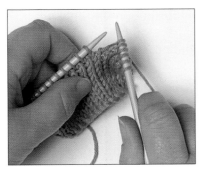

5. Slide your right needle to the right, slipping the used loop on the tip of your left needle off the needle.

6. An extra stitch is now positioned on your right needle just to the right of this last worked stitch.

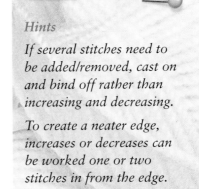

Hints

If several stitches need to be added/removed, cast on and bind off rather than increasing and decreasing.

To create a neater edge, increases or decreases can be worked one or two stitches in from the edge.

shaping basic stitches and techniques

Increasing: Yarn Over While Working Purl Stitch

This method is simply the reverse of "make one on knit row." It will also create a hole in your knitted fabric.

1. Purl to the position for the increase. Take the yarn to the back between the two needles.

2. Insert the tip of your right needle from right to left into the first stitch on your left needle as you would for a purl stitch.

3. Beginning with the yarn at the back, wrap it from right to left (counterclockwise) around the tip of your right needle.

4. Draw the tip of your right needle back through the stitch on your left needle. Keep the wrapped yarn on your right needle.

5. Slide your right needle to the right, slipping the used loop on the tip of your left needle off the needle.

6. An extra stitch is now positioned on your right needle just to the right of this last worked stitch.

7. When working the new stitch in the next row (a knit row), knit into the back of the stitch.

Decreasing: Knitting Two Stitches Together

1. At the position for the decrease, take your right needle from left to right through the front of the first two stitches on your left needle. The tip of your right needle will end up behind your left needle.

2. Wrap the yarn from back to front between the tips of your two needles.

3. Draw the tip of your right needle back through the two stitches on your left needle. Keep the wrapped yarn on your right needle.

4. The wrapped yarn will form a new stitch on your right needle.

5. Slide your right needle to the right, slipping the used loops on the tip of your left needle off the needle.

Decreasing: Purling Two Stitches Together

1. At the position for the decrease, take your right needle from right to left through the fronts of the first two stitches on your left needle. The tip of your right needle will end up in front of your left needle.

2. Wrap the yarn from right to left (counterclockwise) around the tip of your right needle.

3. Draw the tip of your right needle back through the two stitches on your left needle. Keep the wrapped yarn on your right needle.

4. The wrapped yarn will form a new stitch on your right needle.

5. Slide your right needle to the right, slipping the used loops on the tip of your left needle off the needle.

Purling two stitches together

Decreasing: Slip, Slip, Knit

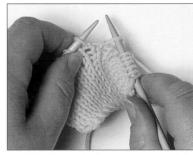

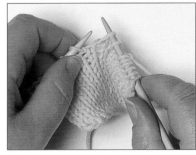

1. At the position for the decrease, insert your right needle into the front of the first stitch on your left needle as you would for a knit stitch.

2. Slip the stitch from your left needle to your right.

3. Repeat steps 1–2 with the next stitch on your left needle.

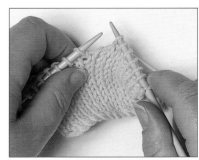

4. Take the tip of your left needle from left to right through the front of the two slipped stitches on your right needle. Your left needle is in front of your right needle.

5. Wrap the yarn from back to front between your two needles.

6. Complete the knit stitch, slipping both used loops on the tip of your left needle off the needle.

basic stitches and techniques shaping

46

Decreasing: Slip, Knit, Pass the Slipped Stitch Over

Slip, slip, knit

1. At the position for the decrease, take your right needle from left to right through the front of the first stitch on your left needle.

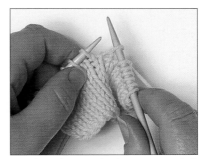

2. Slip the stitch from your left needle to your right.

3. Take your right needle from left to right through the front of the next stitch. Wrap the yarn from back to front between the tips of your two needles.

4. Complete the knit stitch.

5. Take the tip of your left needle from left to right through the front of the slipped stitch (the second stitch from the end on your right needle).

6. Lift the stitch over the knit stitch and the tip of your right needle.

7. Slide the stitch off your left needle and allow it to drop.

Holding Stitches

There are occasions, such as shaping a neckline or pocket opening, when some stitches need to be safely set aside so that you can use them later. See page 13 for information about stitch holders.

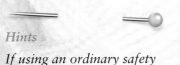

Hints

If using an ordinary safety pin, take care not to split the yarn with the pin's sharp point.

When holding stitches on a length of yarn, use a smooth yarn. It is easier to thread the stitches onto and then off the yarn.

Holding Stitches in a Straight Line

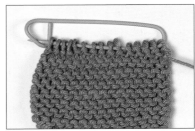

1. Open your chosen stitch holder. Pass the stitches off the needle and onto the stitch holder without twisting them.

2. Close the holder and set the stitches aside.

Holding Stitches in a Curve

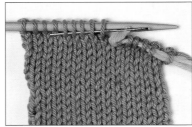

1. Thread a large tapestry needle with a length of contrasting yarn. Take the tapestry needle from right to left through the stitches on the knitting needle.

2. When the required number of stitches is on the spare piece of yarn, tie the ends of the yarn together.

Picking Up Stitches

Whenever you add a border, such as a neckband or collar, the stitches you need to use are generally picked up from the edge of the garment. Stitches can be picked up from horizontal, vertical, and curved edges. Often you will need to use a combination of the following methods.

Hints

Pick up stitches with a crochet hook or a knitting needle that is one to two sizes smaller than the needles you have used for the garment.

To help ensure that you pick up stitches evenly, mark the edge of the knitting at 2" (5 cm) intervals. Use pins or short lengths of yarn as markers.

Occasionally you will need to pick up more stitches than the pattern requires to prevent holes appearing in your work. Pick up the additional stitches and then decrease them in the next row.

If you intend to knit the band in a different color to the main knitting, pick up the stitches using the same yarn as the main knitting. Change to the new color at the beginning of the first row.

Marking the edge

Different color band

Picking Up Stitches along a Bound-Off Edge: Horizontal

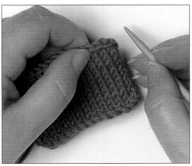

1. Hold the knitted fabric in your left hand with the right side of the fabric facing you. Hold the knitting needle in your right hand.

2. Take your needle from front to back through the center of the first stitch in the row just below the bind off.

3. Starting from the back and leaving a tail at least 4" (10 cm) long, wrap the yarn from right to left (counterclockwise) around the tip of your needle.

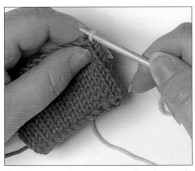

4. Draw the needle backward, pulling the looped yarn to the front to create the first new stitch.

5. Take your needle from front to back through the center of the second stitch in the row just below the bind off.

6. Wrap the yarn as before and pull the loop through to the front.

7. Continue across the edge, picking up a new stitch through the center of each stitch in the row below the bound-off edge.

8. Secure the tail of thread at the beginning of the row (see pages 36–37).

Picking Up Stitches along a Selvage: Vertical

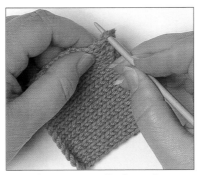

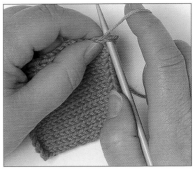

1. Hold the knitted fabric in your left hand with the right side of the fabric facing you and the side edge at the top. Hold the knitting needle in your right hand.

2. Take your needle from front to back between the first and second stitch in the first row.

3. Starting from the back and leaving a tail at least 4" (10 cm) long, wrap the yarn from right to left (counterclockwise) around the tip of your needle.

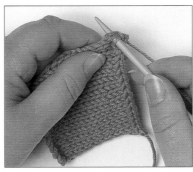

4. Draw the needle backward, pulling the looped yarn to the front to create the first new stitch.

5. Take your needle from front to back between the first and second stitch in the second row.

6. Wrap the yarn as before and pull the loop through to the front.

7. Continue along the edge, occasionally skipping one row to help prevent the new section of knitting from flaring out.

8. Secure the tail of thread at the beginning of the row (see pages 36–37).

Picking Up Stitches along a Curve

1. Hold the knitted fabric in your left hand with the right side of the fabric facing you. Hold the knitting needle in your right hand.

2. Take your needle from front to back through the center of the first stitch one row below the decreasing row.

3. Starting from the back and leaving a tail at least 4" (10 cm) long, wrap the yarn from right to left (counterclockwise) around the tip of your needle.

4. Draw the needle backward, pulling the looped yarn to the front to create the first new stitch.

5. Take your needle from front to back through the center of the next stitch one row below the decreasing row.

6. Wrap the yarn as before and pull the loop through to the front.

7. Continue along the edge, following the curve.

8. Secure the tail of thread at the beginning of the row (see pages 36–37).

Working Short Rows
Working short rows is also known as turning.
The number of stitches of your knitted piece remains the same.

Short Row Shaping While Working Knit Stitch

Hints

This method allows you to create continuous sloped edges and is particularly useful for shaping darts, collars, and shoulders.

Picking up the wrap on the return row and stitching it together with the next stitch ensures that the wrap will become invisible.

1. Knit to the place where your knitted fabric is to be turned. Keeping the yarn at the back, take the tip of your right needle from right to left through the front of the next stitch on your left needle (purlwise).

2. Slip the stitch off your left needle and onto your right needle.

3. Bring the yarn to the front between the two needles.

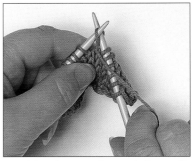

4. Take the tip of your left needle from left to right through the slipped stitch on your right needle.

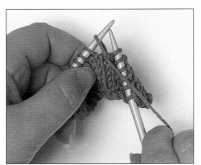

5. Slip the stitch off your right needle and back onto your left needle. The yarn is now wrapped around this stitch.

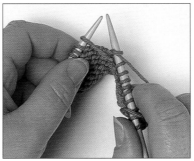

6. Turn your work around. Bring the yarn to the front between the two needles.

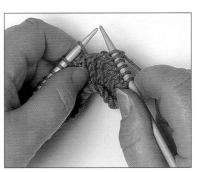

7. Purl to the end of the row. Turn your work around and knit to just before the wrapped stitch.

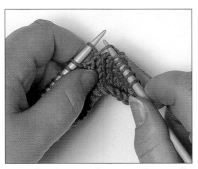

8. Take the tip of your right needle under the front of the wrap.

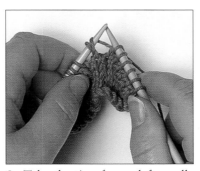

9. Take the tip of your left needle from left to right behind the front of the wrap and slip it onto your left needle.

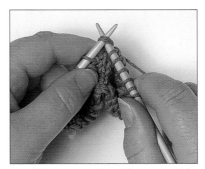

10. Take the tip of your right needle from left to right through both the wrap and the next stitch on your left needle.

11. Complete the knit stitch, working the wrap and stitch together.

12. Continue knitting to the end of the row.

Short Row Shaping While Working Purl Stitch

1. Purl to the place where your knitted fabric is to be turned. Keeping the yarn at the front, take the tip of your right needle from right to left through the front of the next stitch on your left needle (purlwise).

2. Slip the stitch off your left needle and onto your right needle.

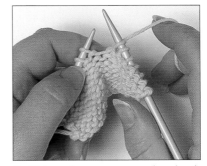

3. Take the yarn to the back between the two needles.

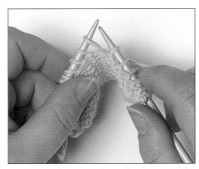

4. Take the tip of your left needle from left to right through the slipped stitch on your right needle.

5. Slip the stitch off your right needle and back onto your left needle. The yarn is now wrapped around this stitch.

6. Turn your work around. Take the yarn to the back between the two needles.

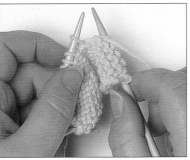

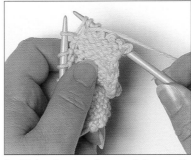

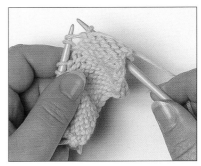

7. Knit to the end of the row. Turn your work around and purl to just before the wrapped stitch.

8. Take the tip of your right needle from right to left through the back of the wrap.

9. Place the wrap on your left needle.

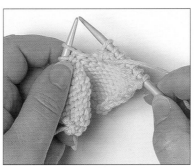

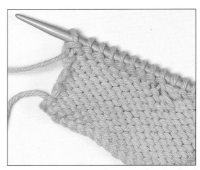

10. Take the tip of your right needle from right to left through both the wrap and the next stitch on your left needle.

11. Complete the purl stitch, working the wrap and the stitch together.

12. Continue purling to the end of the row.

basic stitches and techniques working short rows

Rib Stitches
Rib stitch has more elasticity than garter or stockinette stitch and is the most commonly used stitch for borders and bands. It also creates an edge that does not curl.

Single Rib Stitch: K1, P1

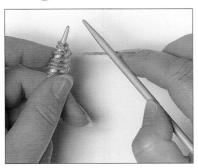

1. After casting on the required number of stitches, hold your needle with the stitches in your left hand. Hold your empty needle and yarn with your right hand (see page 17).

2. With the yarn at the back, work the first stitch as a knit stitch.

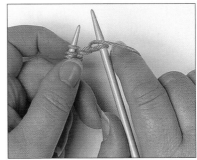

3. Bring the yarn to the front between the tips of your two needles.

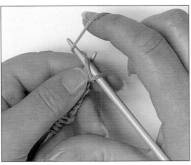

4. Work the next stitch as a purl stitch.

5. Take the yarn to the back between the two needles.

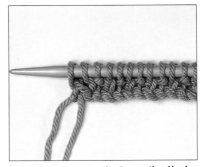

6. Repeat steps 2–5 until all the stitches are on your right needle.

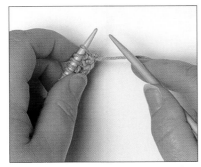

7. Swap the needles over so that the needle with the stitches on it is in your left hand and the empty needle is in your right.

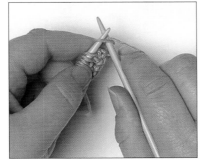

8. If you have an **even number of stitches,** work the first stitch as a knit stitch.

9. Continue across the row in the same manner as before.

rib stitches basic stitches and techniques

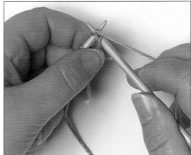

10. Work every row in exactly the same manner.

11. If you have an **odd number of stitches,** work the first stitch as a purl stitch.

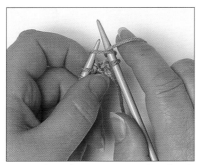

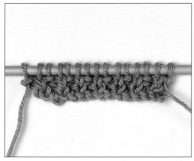

12. Take the yarn to the back between the two needles and work the second stitch as a knit stitch.

13. Continue across the row in the same manner as before, alternating between purl and knit stitches.

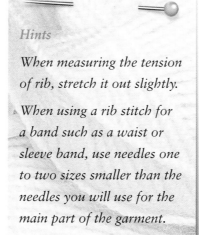

14. Work the required number of rows, alternating between starting each row with a knit stitch or a purl stitch.

Hints

When measuring the tension of rib, stretch it out slightly.

When using a rib stitch for a band such as a waist or sleeve band, use needles one to two sizes smaller than the needles you will use for the main part of the garment.

Single rib stitch

Double rib stitch

basic stitches and techniques rib stitches

Double Rib Stitch: **K2, P2**

This rib stitch is best worked over an even number of stitches. It looks the same on both sides of the fabric.

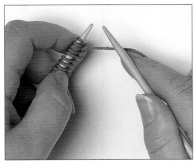

1. After casting on the required number of stitches, hold your needle with the stitches in your left hand. Hold your empty needle and yarn with your right hand (see page 17).

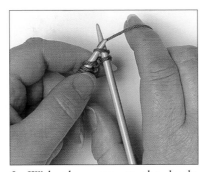

2. With the yarn at the back, work the first two stitches as knit stitches.

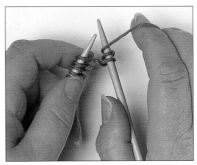

3. Bring the yarn to the front between the tips of your two needles.

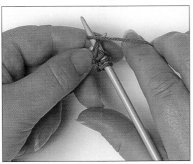

4. Work the next two stitches as purl stitches.

5. Take the yarn to the back between the two needles.

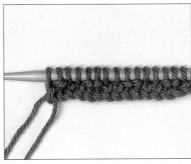

6. Repeat steps 2–5 until all the stitches are on your right needle.

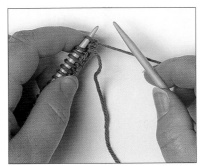

7. Swap the needles over so that the needle with the stitches on it is in your left hand and the empty needle is in your right.

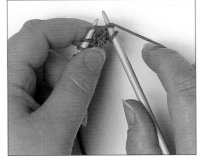

8. If the previous row **finished with two purl stitches,** begin the next row with two knit stitches.

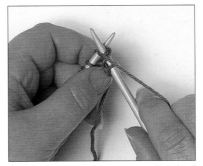

9. If the previous row **finished with two knit stitches,** begin the next row with two purl stitches.

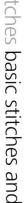

rib stitches basic stitches and techniques

10. Continue across the row, alternating between two purl stitches and two knit stitches.

11. Work this row and all subsequent rows in exactly the same manner.

12. Work the required number of rows, alternating between starting each row with two knit stitches or two purl stitches.

Other Rib Stitches
Different combinations of knit and purl can be used to create a wide variety of rib patterns.

Knit 5, Purl 2—K5, P2

For this rib, the number of stitches must be a multiple of seven, plus five. Alternate the following two rows.

Row 1: Knit 5, purl 2. Repeat this to the last 5 stitches. Knit 5.

Row 2: Purl 5, knit 2. Repeat this to the last 5 stitches. Purl 5.

Broken Double Rib

This creates a firmer fabric. An even number of stitches is required. Alternate the following two rows.

Row 1: Knit 2, purl 2. Repeat this to the end of the row.

Row 2: Purl across the entire row.

Knit 2, Purl 5—K2, P5

This rib is the reverse of the previous rib. Again, the number of stitches must be a multiple of seven, plus five. Alternate the following two rows.

Row 1: Purl 5, knit 2. Repeat this to the last 5 stitches. Purl 5.

Row 2: Knit 5, purl 2. Repeat this to the last 5 stitches. Knit 5.

Single Twisted Rib

Knitting and purling through the back of the loops creates a twist in the stitches. With an even number of stitches, alternate the following two rows.

Row 1: Knit 1 through the back of the loop, purl 1. Repeat this to the end of the row.

Row 2: Purl 1 through the back of the loop, knit 1. Repeat this to the end of the row.

Making Buttonholes

Small, round buttonhole while working in knit stitch

Large, round buttonhole while working in knit stitch

Small, round buttonhole while working in purl stitch

Large, round buttonhole while working in purl stitch

Vertical buttonhole—slipping stitches

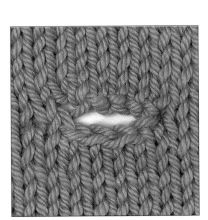

Horizontal buttonhole—slipping stitches

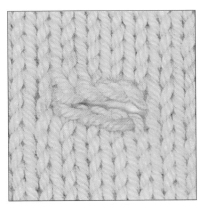

Horizontal buttonhole—casting on and binding off

Damask Rose by Jenny Brown

Small, Round Buttonhole While Working in Knit Stitch

Round buttonholes are also known as eyelet buttonholes.

1. Knit to the position for the buttonhole. Bring the yarn to the front between your two needles.

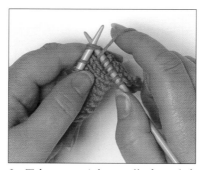

2. Take your right needle from left to right behind the front of the first two stitches on your left needle.

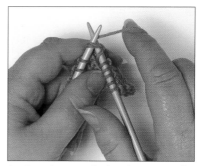

3. Starting and finishing at the front, wrap the yarn from right to left (counterclockwise) around your right needle.

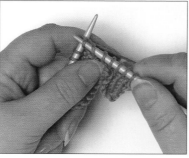

4. Draw the tip of your right needle back through the two stitches on your left needle. Keep the wrapped yarn on your right needle.

5. Slide your right needle to the right, slipping the used loops on the tip of your left needle off the needle.

6. Finish the row. On the next row, knit or purl the yarn over according to your pattern to complete the buttonhole.

Large, Round Buttonhole While Working in Knit Stitch

1. Knit to the position for the buttonhole. Bring the yarn to the front between your two needles.

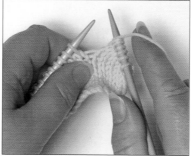

2. Starting and finishing at the front, wrap the yarn from right to left (counterclockwise) around your right needle.

3. Insert your right needle from left to right into the front of the first two stitches on your left needle.

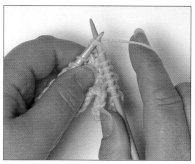

4. Starting and finishing at the front, wrap the yarn from right to left (counterclockwise) around your right needle.

5. Draw the tip of your right needle back through the two stitches on your left needle. Keep the wrapped yarn on your right needle.

6. Slide your right needle to the right, slipping the used loops on the tip of your left needle off the needle.

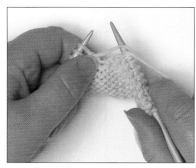

7. Finish the row. On the next row, knit or purl according to your pattern up to the yarn overs.

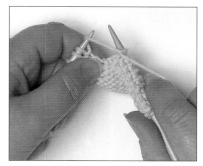

8. According to your pattern, knit or purl the first yarn over.

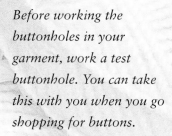

Hints

Before working the buttonholes in your garment, work a test buttonhole. You can take this with you when you go shopping for buttons.

It is better to make buttonholes a little too small rather than a little too large because the knitting will stretch over time.

Knitted buttonholes can be reinforced with blanket or overcast stitches.

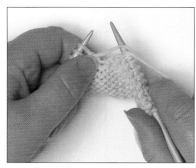

9. Allow the second yarn over to drop off your left needle without stitching into it.

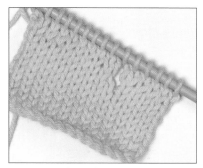

10. Complete the row. Turn and stitch the next row according to your pattern to complete the buttonhole.

making buttonholes basic stitches and techniques

Small, Round Buttonhole While Working in Purl Stitch

1. Purl to the position for the buttonhole. Wrap the yarn once around your right needle in a counterclockwise direction.

2. Take your right needle from right to left behind the front of the first two stitches on your left needle.

3. Starting and finishing at the front, wrap the yarn from right to left (counterclockwise) around your right needle.

4. Draw the tip of your right needle back through the two stitches on your left needle. Keep the wrapped yarn on your right needle.

5. Slide your right needle to the right, slipping the used loops on the tip of your left needle off the needle.

6. Finish the row. On the next row, knit or purl the yarnover according to your pattern to complete the buttonhole.

Large, Round Buttonhole While Working in Purl Stitch

1. Purl to the position for the buttonhole. Wrap the yarn twice around your right needle in a counterclockwise direction.

2. Take your right needle from right to left behind the front of the first two stitches on your left needle.

3. Starting and finishing at the front, wrap the yarn from right to left (counterclockwise) around your right needle.

4. Draw the tip of your right needle back through the two stitches on your left needle. Keep the wrapped yarn on your right needle.

5. Slide your right needle to the right, slipping the used loops on the tip of your left needle off the needle.

6. Finish the row. On the next row, knit or purl according to your pattern up to the yarn overs.

7. According to your pattern, knit or purl the first yarn over.

8. Allow the second yarn over to drop off your left needle without stitching into it.

9. Complete the row. Turn and stitch the next row according to your pattern to complete the buttonhole.

Vertical Buttonhole: Slipping Stitches

1. Stitch to the position for the buttonhole.

2. Turn your work around.

3. Transfer the stitches on the other side of the buttonhole onto a stitch holder. Stitch back across the section of stitches you worked in the last row.

making buttonholes basic stitches and techniques

4. Continue working rows on the same side of the buttonhole as before until you reach the desired buttonhole height. Finish at the edge of the buttonhole and leave the yarn dangling.

5. Turn your work around. Transfer the held stitches back onto a needle.

6. Join in a new yarn on the second side of the buttonhole. Continue working rows across the stitches on the second side of the buttonhole until you have one row less than on the first side.

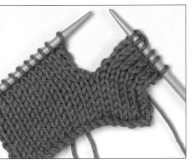

7. Turn your work around. Cut the yarn, leaving a tail at least 4" (10 cm) long.

8. Pick up the yarn from the first side. Continue stitching across the stitches on the second side.

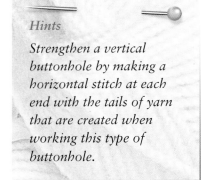

Hints

Strengthen a vertical buttonhole by making a horizontal stitch at each end with the tails of yarn that are created when working this type of buttonhole.

9. When you have completed the piece, thread one tail of yarn into a tapestry needle. Work a horizontal stitch across the end of the buttonhole.

10. Finish off the tail of yarn. Thread the tail of yarn at the opposite end of the buttonhole into the tapestry needle and repeat the procedure.

Enigma by Christine Wood and Cara Seppelt

basic stitches and techniques **making buttonholes**

Horizontal Buttonhole: Slipping Stitches

1. Stitch to the position for the buttonhole. Bring the yarn to the front.

2. Take the tip of your right needle from left to right into the front of the next stitch on your left needle.

3. Slip the stitch from your left needle to your right needle.

4. Take the yarn to the back.

5. Take the tip of your right needle from left to right into the front of the next stitch on your left needle.

6. Slip the stitch from your left needle to your right needle.

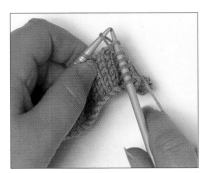

7. Pick up the first slipped stitch with your left needle.

8. Pass the stitch over the second slipped stitch and off the tip of your right needle.

9. Remove the tip of your left needle from the stitch and allow it to drop between the needles.

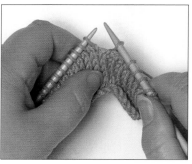

10. Keeping the yarn at the back, repeat steps 5–9 until the buttonhole is one stitch shorter than the required width.

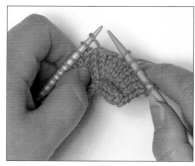

11. Pass the last stitch on your right needle back onto your left needle.

12. Turn your work around.

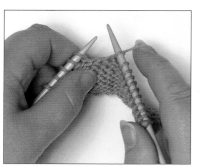

13. Take the yarn to the back.

14. Using the cable cast-on method (see pages 19–20), firmly cast-on one more stitch than the number you decreased.

15. Turn your work around.

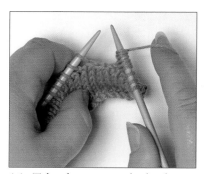

16. Take the yarn to the back.

17. Take the tip of your right needle from left to right into the front of the next two stitches on your left needle.

18. Knit these two stitches together and continue to the end of the row, following your pattern.

basic stitches and techniques making buttonholes

66

Horizontal Buttonhole: Casting On and Binding Off

This method creates a buttonhole that is not as firm as the slip-stitch method.

1. Stitch to the position for the buttonhole. Knit the next two stitches.

2. Take the tip of your left needle from left to right into the front of the first of these two stitches on your right needle.

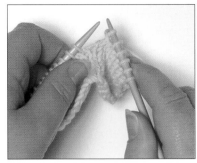

3. Take the stitch over the second stitch and off your right needle, dropping it off your left needle as well.

4. Knit the next stitch on your left needle.

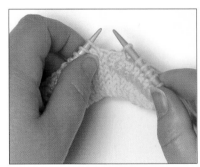

5. Repeat steps 2–3 to bind off the next stitch.

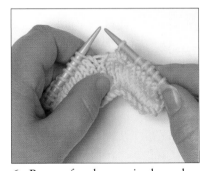

6. Repeat for the required number of stitches.

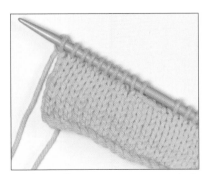

7. According to your pattern, knit or purl to the end of the row.

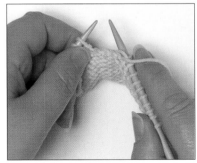

8. On the next row, knit or purl according to your pattern up to the buttonhole.

9. Turn your knitting around.

10. Take the tip of your right needle from front to back behind the first stitch on your left needle.

11. Wrap the yarn around the tip of your right needle in a counter-clockwise direction. Pull the yarn downward between your two needles until it rests on the first stitch.

12. Draw your right needle backward. As you reach the tip, twist it to pick up the yarn between your needles.

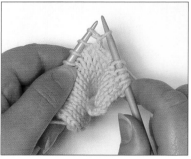

13. Pull the yarn through, forming a loop on your right needle.

14. Take your left needle from right to left through the loop on your right needle.

15. Remove your right needle from the loop. There is now an extra stitch on your left needle.

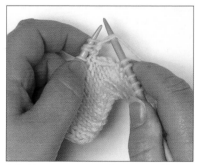

16. Repeat steps 10–15 until you have cast on the same number of stitches that you bound off. Before placing the last cast on onto your left needle, bring the yarn to the front (this prevents an unsightly loop from forming).

17. Turn your knitting around again.

18. According to your pattern, knit or purl to the end of the row.

basic stitches and techniques making buttonholes

Fixing Mistakes

The wonderful thing about knitting is that no matter what has gone wrong, there is usually a ready solution. Whether you are a beginner or an experienced knitter, there is nothing surer than at some point you will have a mistake to fix.

Untwisting a Knit Stitch

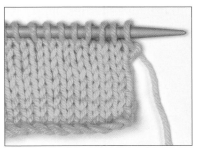

1. The fourth stitch from the right is twisted. Note how the front of the stitch sits further to the left than the back of the stitch.

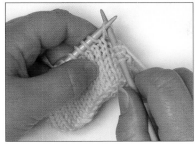

2. Knit up to the stitch. Take the tip of your right needle from right to left through the back of the loop.

3. Wrap the yarn from back to front between the needles.

A twisted stitch can occur if you pick up a dropped stitch and place it back on your needle the wrong way or if you have incorrectly wrapped the yarn on the previous row.

4. Complete the knit stitch.

Untwisting a Purl Stitch

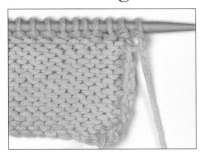

1. The fourth stitch from the right is twisted. Note how the front of the stitch sits further to the left than the back of the stitch.

2. Purl up to the stitch. Take the tip of your right needle from right to left through the back of the loop.

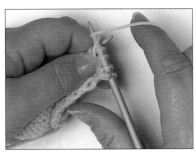

3. Wrap the yarn from right to left (counterclockwise) around the tip of your right needle.

4. Complete the purl stitch.

Picking Up a Dropped Stitch

There are various ways to pick up a dropped stitch. The method you choose will largely depend on how soon you discover the offending stitch.

Picking Up a Knit Stitch from the Previous Row

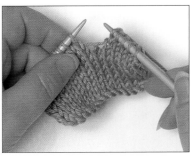

1. Stitch to the position of the dropped stitch. Ensure the loose section of yarn is behind the loop of the dropped stitch.

2. Take your right needle from front to back through the loop of the dropped stitch and then take it under the loose section of yarn.

3. Take the tip of your left needle from left to right through the dropped stitch on your right needle.

4. Lift the stitch back over the loose section of yarn and off your right needle.

5. Take the tip of your left needle from right to left through the front of the stitch on your right needle.

6. Draw back your right needle, slipping the stitch off your right needle and leaving it on your left needle.

7. Knit the picked up stitch and continue working across the row.

Picking Up a Purl Stitch from the Previous Row

1. Stitch to the position of the dropped stitch. Ensure the loose section of yarn is in front of the loop of the dropped stitch.

basic stitches and techniques fixing mistakes

2. Take your right needle from right to left through the loop of the dropped stitch and then take it under the loose section of yarn.

3. Take the tip of your left needle from left to right through the dropped stitch on your right needle.

4. Lift the stitch back over the loose section of yarn and off your right needle.

5. Drop the loop off your left needle. Take the tip of your left needle from left to right through the back of the stitch on your right needle.

6. Draw back your right needle, slipping the stitch off your right needle and leaving it on your left needle.

7. Purl the picked up stitch and continue working across the row.

Picking Up a Knit Stitch from Several Rows Below

1. Stitch to the position of the dropped stitch. Ensure the loose sections of yarn are behind the loop of the dropped stitch.

2. Insert a crochet hook from front to back through the loop of the dropped stitch.

3. Catch the first loose section of yarn with your crochet hook.

fixing mistakes basic stitches and techniques

4. Pull the loose strand from back to front through the loop.

5. Catch the next loose section of yarn with your crochet hook.

6. Pull this loose strand through the loop on the crochet hook in the same manner as before.

7. Continue in the same manner until no more loose sections remain.

8. Take the tip of your left needle from left to right through the front of the stitch on your crochet hook.

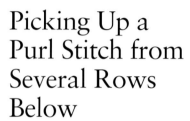

Picking Up a Purl Stitch from Several Rows Below

It is easier to turn your work around and pick up the stitch as for a knit stitch.

9. Transfer the loop onto your left needle.

10. Knit the picked up stitch and continue working across the row.

Unraveling Stitch by Stitch: Knit Stitches

1. With the stitches on your right needle and your left needle empty, keep the yarn to the back.

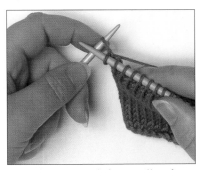

2. Take your left needle from left to right through the back of the first stitch one row below the stitches on your right needle.

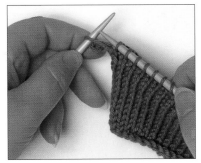

3. Draw back your right needle, dropping a stitch off your right needle while keeping the stitch below on your left needle.

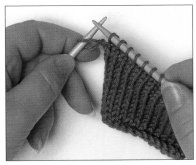

4. Pull the yarn at the back.

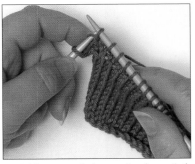

5. Take your left needle from left to right through the back of the next stitch one row below the stitches on your right needle.

6. Transfer the stitch to your left needle and drop the stitch above from your right needle in the same manner as before.

7. Continue in the same manner for the required number of stitches.

Hints

Check and recheck your knitting often. The sooner you pick up a mistake the easier it is to fix it.

Pick up dropped stitches as soon as you find them or they will continue to unravel farther down your knitting.

fixing mistakes basic stitches and techniques

Unraveling Stitch by Stitch: Purl Stitches

1. With the stitches on your right needle and your left needle empty, keep the yarn to the front.

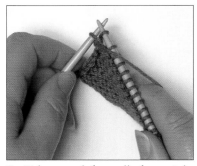

2. Take your left needle from right to left through the front of the first stitch one row below the stitches on your right needle.

3. Draw back your right needle, dropping a stitch off your right needle while keeping the stitch below on your left needle.

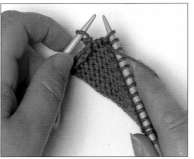

4. Pull the yarn at the front.

5. Take your left needle from right to left through the front of the next stitch one row below the stitches on your right needle.

Hints

Grafting can also be used to correct mistakes (see pages 143–144).

If you have made a mistake in multicolored knitting, Swiss darning can be used to alter stitches of the wrong color (see pages 131–132).

6. Transfer the stitch to your left needle and drop the stitch above from your right needle in the same manner as before.

7. Continue in the same manner for the required number of stitches.

Unraveling Multiple Rows and Picking Up with Knit Stitch Unraveling is easy. It is the picking up of the stitches that needs a little care.

Method 1

1. Take all the stitches off the needle.

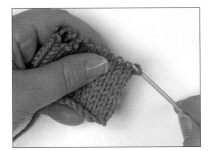

2. Pull the yarn until the top row of stitches is one row below the mistake you wish to correct. Ensure the yarn is on the left-hand side.

3. Beginning on the right hand side and using a smaller needle, take your needle from right to left (and back to front) through the first stitch on the right.

Use method 2 if you are concerned about unraveling too many rows.

Method 2

4. Continue picking up all the stitches in the same manner.

1. Working one row below the mistake you wish to correct and beginning on the right-hand side with a smaller needle, take the needle from right to left behind the right half of the first stitch.

2. Take the needle behind the right half of the second stitch in the same manner.

3. Continue in this manner until the needle has passed through all the stitches in the row.

4. Remove the needle at the top of the work.

5. Pull the yarn to unravel all the stitches above the smaller needle.

Unraveling Multiple Rows and Picking Up with Purl Stitch

Method 1

1. Take all the stitches off the needle.

2. Pull the yarn until the top row of stitches is one row below the mistake you wish to correct. Ensure the yarn is on the left-hand side.

Method 2

3. Beginning on the right-hand side and using a smaller needle, take it from right to left (and back to front) through the first stitch on the right.

4. Continue picking up all the stitches in the same manner.

1. Work one row below the mistake you wish to correct. Begin on the right-hand side with a smaller needle and take it from right to left behind the vertical right half of the first stitch.

2. Take the needle behind the vertical right half of the second stitch in the same manner.

3. Continue in this manner until the needle has passed through all the stitches in the row.

4. Remove the needle at the top of the work.

5. Pull the yarn to unravel all the stitches above the smaller needle.

And Then There's More
Aran Knitting

Aran knitting is thought to have originated in the Aran Islands—a group of three islands just off the west coast of Ireland. Originally made with undyed cream sheep's wool, Aran-style knitting featured complex patterns created with cables, twists, and bobbles. These techniques can be used to create an enormous range of interesting patterns.

Hints

Use a cable needle that is slightly smaller than your knitting needles so that you do not stretch the stitches.

If you use a cable needle with a bend in the middle, you will be less likely to lose your stitches.

Cables

Crossing one group of stitches over or under another group creates cables. A cable needle is used to hold the stitches on either the right or wrong side of the knitted fabric.

Cables to the left

Cable to the Left

We have used a cable that is six stitches wide.

1. Work the cable in stockinette stitch and the background in reverse stockinette stitch, finishing with a wrong-side row.

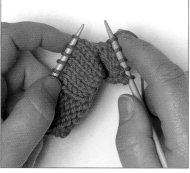

2. Turn your work to the right side. Stitch to the position of the crossover. Take the yarn to the back.

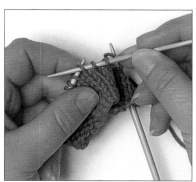

3. With the cable needle at the front, slip half of the cable stitches, one by one (in this instance, three stitches), onto the needle purlwise.

4. Keeping the cable needle at the front, knit the remaining cable stitches (three stitches).

5. Slide the stitches on the cable needle toward the right-hand tip.

6. Knit the first stitch that was slipped onto the cable needle.

7. Knit the remaining stitches on the cable needle. The cable twists to the left.

8. Complete the row following your pattern.

9. Work the required number of rows up to the position for the next crossover, finishing with a wrong-side row. (We have worked seven more rows.)

10. Repeat steps 2–8 to form a second crossover. Continue in the same manner for the desired length.

Cable to the Right We have used a cable that is six stitches wide.

1. Work the cable in stockinette stitch and the background in reverse stockinette stitch, finishing with a wrong-side row.

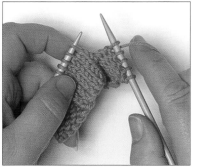

2. Turn your work to the right side. Stitch to the position of the crossover. Take the yarn to the back.

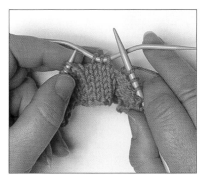

3. With the cable needle at the back, slip half of the cable stitches, one by one (in this instance, three stitches), onto the needle purlwise.

and then there's more aran knitting

4. Keeping the cable needle at the back, knit the remaining cable stitches (three stitches).

5. Slide the stitches on the cable needle toward the right-hand tip.

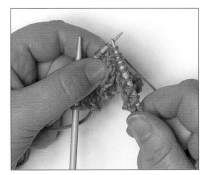

6. Knit the first stitch that was slipped onto the cable needle.

7. Knit the remaining stitches on the cable needle. The cable twists to the right.

8. Complete the row following your pattern.

Cables to the right

9. Work the required number of rows up to the position for the next crossover, finishing with a wrong-side row. (We have worked seven more rows.)

10. Repeat steps 2–8 to form a second crossover. Continue in the same manner for the desired length.

aran knitting and then there's more

79

Twists

When working twists, the stitches are worked out of sequence in the same way that they are when making cables, but a cable needle is not used.

Twist to the Left

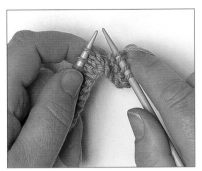

1. With the right side of your work facing you, knit to the position for the twist.

2. Skip the next stitch on your left needle and take your right needle from right to left through the back of the second stitch.

3. Wrap the yarn counterclockwise around the tip of your right needle.

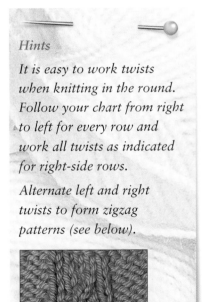

Hints

It is easy to work twists when knitting in the round. Follow your chart from right to left for every row and work all twists as indicated for right-side rows.

Alternate left and right twists to form zigzag patterns (see below).

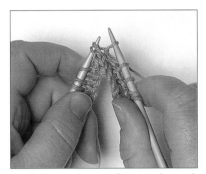

4. Pull the loop of yarn through but leave the stitch on your left needle.

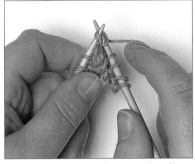

5. Take your right needle from right to left through the back of both the first and second stitches on your left needle.

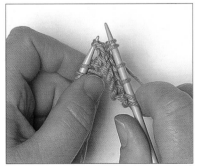

6. Knit the two stitches together.

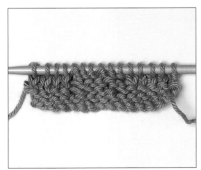

7. Complete the row following your pattern. Turn your work and complete the next row.

and then there's more aran knitting

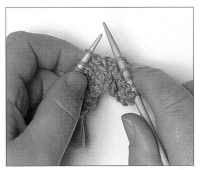

8. Turn your work. Knit to the position for the twist. This will be one stitch to the left of the previous twist.

9. Repeat steps 2–6.

10. Complete the row. Continue working twists in every right-side row, placing them one stitch to the left of the previous twist. A diagonal line to the left will form.

Twist to the Right Method 1

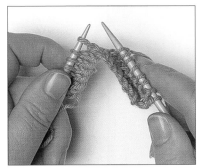

1. With the right side of your work facing you, knit to the position for the twist.

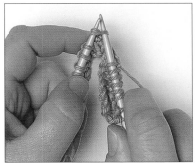

2. Take your right needle from left to right through the front of the second stitch on your left needle.

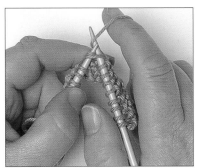

3. Wrap the yarn counterclockwise around the tip of your right needle.

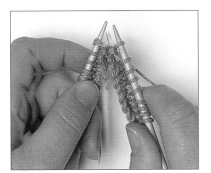

4. Pull the loop of yarn through with your right needle but leave the stitch on your left needle.

5. Take your right needle from right to left through the back of the first stitch on your left needle.

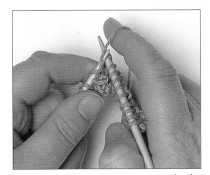

6. Wrap the yarn counterclockwise around the tip of your right needle.

aran knitting and then there's more

81

7. Pull the loop of yarn through with your right needle and drop both the first and second stitches from your left needle.

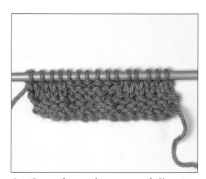

8. Complete the row following your pattern. Turn your work and complete the next row.

9. Turn your work. Knit to the position for the twist. This will be one stitch to the right of the previous twist.

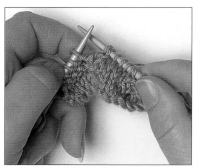

10. Repeat steps 2–7.

11. Complete the row. Continue working twists in every right-side row, placing them one stitch to the right of the previous twist. A diagonal line to the right will form.

Twist to the Right Method 2

1. With the right side of your work facing you, knit to the position for the twist.

2. Take your right needle from left to right through the front of the first two stitches on your left needle (knitwise).

3. Wrap the yarn counterclockwise around the tip of your right needle.

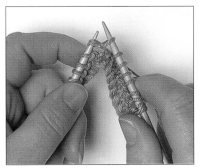

4. Pull the loop of yarn through with your right needle but leave both stitches on your left needle.

5. Take your right needle from left to right through the front of the first stitch on your left needle.

6. Wrap the yarn counterclockwise around the tip of your right needle.

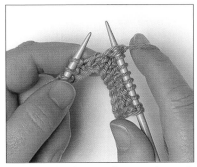

7. Pull the loop of yarn through with your right needle and drop both the first and second stitches from your left needle.

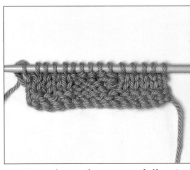

8. Complete the row following your pattern. Turn your work and complete the next row.

9. Turn your work. Knit to the position for the twist. This will be one stitch to the right of the previous twist.

10. Repeat steps 2–7.

11. Complete the row. Continue working twists in every right-side row, placing them one stitch to the right of the previous twist. A diagonal line to the right will form.

aran knitting and then there's more

Bobbles

Bobbles are an interesting way to add texture to your knitting and there are several ways to create them.

Hints

Always start bobbles on right-side rows.

Alter the size of a bobble by varying the number of stitches created and the number of rows you work it over.

Ensure that the first stitch you work after forming a bobble is worked tightly to help hold the bobble in place.

Bobbles can be worked in stockinette stitch, reverse stockinette stitch, or garter stitch.

Method 1

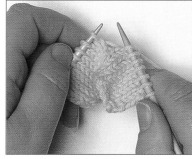

1. With the right side of your work facing you, knit to the position for the bobble.

2. Knit the next stitch but leave it on your left needle.

3. Purl into the same stitch but still leave it on your left needle.

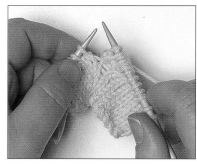

4. Continue working knit one, purl one into the same stitch until you have the required number of stitches. Drop the stitch off your needle after working the last stitch.

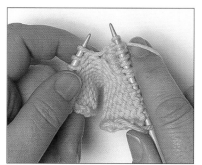

5. Turn your work and knit across the bobble stitches only.

6. Knitting only the bobble stitches, work the desired number of rows, turning your work after each one (altogether, we have worked four rows).

7. Ensure the right side is facing you. Using your left needle, pick up the second stitch of the bobble on your right needle.

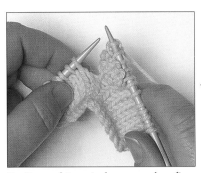

8. Pass this stitch over the first stitch and drop it off your needles.

9. Pick up the "new" second stitch on your right needle.

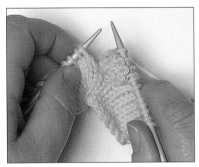

10. Pass this stitch over the first stitch and drop it off your needles.

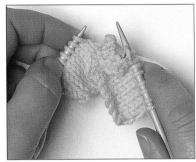

11. Repeat steps 9–10 until only one stitch remains.

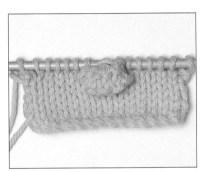

12. Continue working to the end of the row.

Method 2

In this method you do not have to keep turning your work for every row of the bobble.

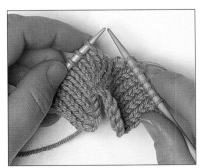

1. With the right side of your work facing you, knit to the position for the bobble.

2. Knit the next stitch but leave it on your left needle.

3. Knit into the back of the same stitch but still leave it on your left needle.

4. Alternate between knitting into the front and then into the back of the same stitch until you have the required number of stitches.

5. Take your left needle from left to right through the front of the first stitch on your right needle.

6. Slip the stitch onto your left needle.

7. Repeat steps 5–6 until all the bobble stitches are on your left needle.

8. Knit across the bobble stitches.

9. Repeat steps 5–8 for the desired number of rows.

10. Bind off the bobble stitches, following method 1 (see page 85).

11. Continue working to the end of the row.

Method 3

1. With the right side of your work facing you, knit to the position for the bobble.

2. Knit the next stitch but leave it on your left needle.

3. Knit into the back of the same stitch but still leave it on your left needle.

4. Alternate between knitting into the front and then into the back of the same stitch until you have the required number of stitches. Drop the stitch off your left needle after working the last stitch.

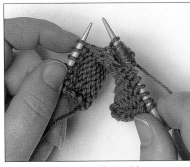

5. Turn your work and knit across the bobble stitches only.

6. Knitting only the bobble stitches, work the desired number of rows, turning your work after each one.

7. Ensure the right side is facing you. Bind off the bobble stitches, following method 1 (see page 85).

8. Continue working to the end of the row.

Beaded Knitting
Threading Beads and Sequins

Beads and sequins need to be threaded onto your knitting yarn before you begin and there are several methods you can use. Choose the method that suits you and your materials the best.

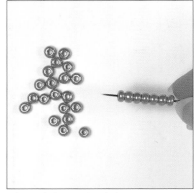

Thread the end of the yarn into a sewing needle and simply scoop up the beads with the tip of the needle.

However, if you cannot pass the yarn through the eye of the needle, try one of the following:

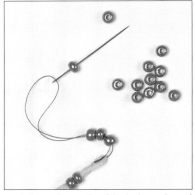

1. Thread a doubled length of sewing thread into a needle. Pass the end of the yarn through the loop of the thread. Scoop up the beads with the needle and then push them along the sewing thread and onto the yarn.

Glittering Dreams by Karen Torrisi

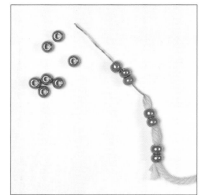

2. Place the end of the yarn over a piece of wire approximately 2" (5 cm) long. Fold the wire over the yarn and twist the two halves of wire together. Thread the beads onto the wire and down onto the yarn.

3. Purchase beads that are already strung. Tie the end of the yarn to the end of the bead string and slide the beads onto the yarn.

and then there's more beaded knitting

Using Beads: Slip Stitch

Hints

Try to thread up with more beads than you will need. If you run out of beads, cut the yarn, thread on more beads, and then rejoin the yarn.

Work the stitches on either side of a bead or sequin very firmly. This will help keep the bead or sequin in place and prevent it from falling to the back.

Avoid placing beads or sequins within your seam allowances.

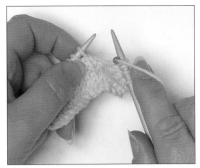

1. On the right side of the knitted fabric, knit to the position for the first bead. Bring the yarn to the front between the tips of the needles.

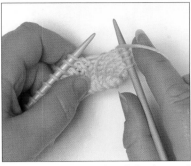

2. Push a bead down the yarn until it rests in front of the next stitch.

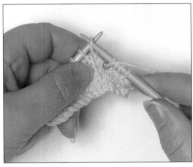

3. Take the tip of your right needle from right to left through the next stitch.

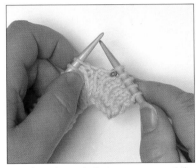

4. Slip the stitch onto your right needle (this is purlwise). Take the yarn to the back between the tips of the needles, leaving the bead in front of the slipped stitch.

5. Continue to the position for the next bead and secure it following steps 2–4.

6. Attach all the remaining beads in the same manner.

Using Sequins: Adding from the Wrong Side

This method can also be used for attaching beads. They will lie at a slight angle along the vertical edge of a stitch.

Hints

Before beginning your garment, test the beads on a knitted swatch to check that they will not make your knitting sag.

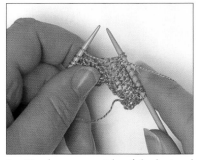

1. On the wrong side of the knitted fabric, purl to the position for the first sequin.

2. Take the tip of your right needle from right to left through the next stitch and wrap the yarn as you would for a purl stitch.

3. Slide a sequin down the yarn until it is level with your right needle.

4. Push the sequin through the stitch and to the back with your left thumb.

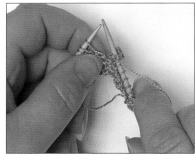

5. Complete the stitch and slip it off your left needle. The sequin is in position on the right side of your fabric.

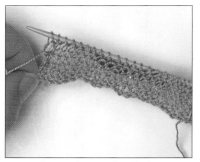

6. Purl to the end of the row, adding sequins where you want them.

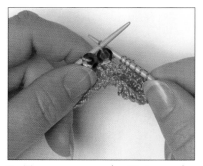

7. Turn your work. Knit to the position of the last added sequin. Take the tip of your right needle from right to left through the back of the next stitch (the one with the sequin in it).

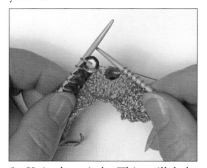

8. Knit the stitch. This will help anchor the sequin in position.

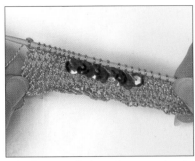

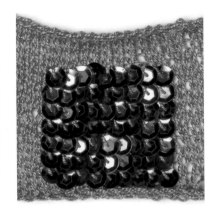

9. Knit to the position of the next sequin and knit into the back of the stitch in the same manner as before.

10. Secure all the other sequins in the row in the same manner.

Circular Knitting (or knitting in the round)

Knitting in the round can be worked with either a set of four or five double-pointed needles or with a circular needle. The double-pointed needles are most useful for small items such as socks and the circular needles for larger items.

With this technique, the right side of the knitted fabric always faces you.

Working on a Set of Four Double-Pointed Needles

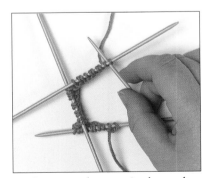

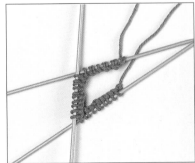

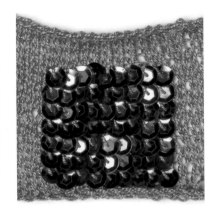

1. Cast on the required number of stitches in the same manner as for straight knitting, dividing them evenly over three needles.

2. Arrange the needles into a triangle. Ensure the stitches are not twisted and that the cast-on edge is to the inside.

3. Hold the needle with the first cast-on stitch in your left hand and the needle with the last cast-on stitch in your right hand.

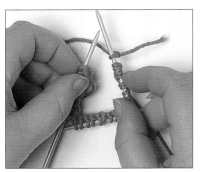

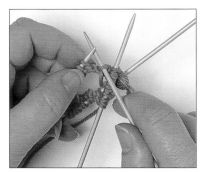

4. Place a marker on the tip of your right needle to indicate the beginning of the row.

5. Using the spare needle, work the first stitch very tightly so that your garment won't gape at this point.

6. Continue stitching across the row until all the stitches on your left needle have been knitted onto the spare needle.

Hints

When using double-pointed needles, work the first stitch on a needle firmly so that your knitting does not gape at these changeover points.

To produce stockinette stitch, work all rows with knit stitch. Alternating rows of knit and purl stitch will produce garter stitch.

If you are working a pattern from a chart, read every row from right to left and omit any edge stitches.

When using a circular needle, ensure it is an appropriate size for the number of stitches you are working with. If it is too long the stitches will become stretched. The needle should be shorter than the finished diameter of your item.

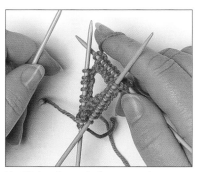

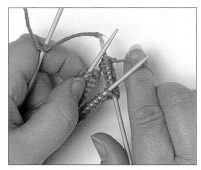

7. Knit the stitches on the next needle onto the empty needle.

8. Repeat the procedure until reaching the row marker. One row is now complete.

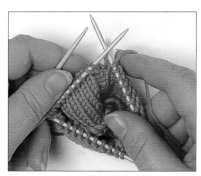

9. Slip the marker from your left needle to your right needle and begin the second row.

10. Continue working all the rows in the same manner.

and then there's more circular knitting

Working on a Circular Needle

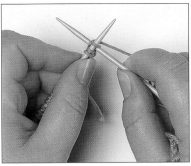

1. Cast on the required number of stitches in the same manner as for straight knitting.

2. Spread the stitches evenly along the entire needle and ensure the stitches are not twisted. Holding the ends of the needle together, turn the cast-on edge to the inside.

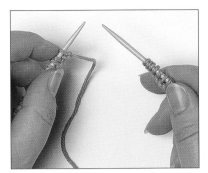

3. Hold the end with the last cast-on stitch in your right hand and the other end in your left hand.

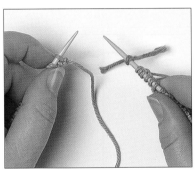

4. Place a marker on the tip of your right needle to indicate the beginning of the row.

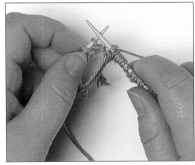

5. Work the first stitch very tightly so that your garment won't gape at this point.

6. Continue stitching across the row until reaching the row marker. Frequently push the stitches along the needle so that they do not become stretched out at any point. One row is now complete.

7. Slip the marker from your left needle to your right needle and begin the second row.

8. Continue working all the rows in the same manner.

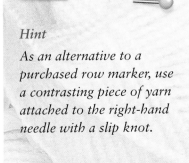

Hint

As an alternative to a purchased row marker, use a contrasting piece of yarn attached to the right-hand needle with a slip knot.

circular knitting and then there's more

Knitting with Multiple Colors

Knitting Stripes

Working horizontal stripes is the easiest way to add different colors to your knitting.

If you work each stripe with an even number of rows, you will be able to carry the yarn up the side of your knitted piece.

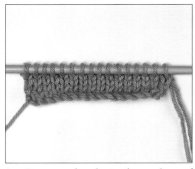

1. Cast on the desired number of stitches. Work the required number of rows with your first yarn color. Join in a new yarn following the instructions on pages 36–37. Do not cut off the yarn you have just been using.

2. Work two rows of your second stripe. Leave the first yarn dangling.

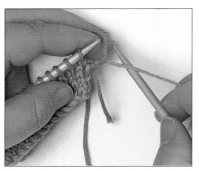

3. At the beginning of the third stripe, pick up the first yarn. Twist it once with the yarn you are using.

4. Continue working your third stripe. Twist the yarns after every second row as in step 3 even if your stripe is thicker than two rows of knitting.

5. Continue working rows and carrying the yarn up the side of your knitting.

Fair Isle Knitting

Fair Isle knitting is the term used to refer to color knitting where generally two, but sometimes more, colors are used in the same row. It is also known as jacquard knitting and stranded knitting. The Shetland Isles, Norway, and South America all have a rich tradition of this type of knitting. The techniques of stranding and weaving are used to accommodate the multiple colors.

Stranding

Stranding is the process of carrying the yarn not currently in use on the back of the fabric for short distances. Only use this method when the yarn is to be carried for four stitches or less.

Stranding on a Knit Row: Holding One Yarn at a Time

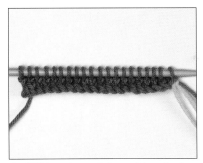

1. With the right side facing you, join the contrast color at the beginning of the row.

2. Drop the contrast yarn and knit to the position for the color change. Spread out the stitches on your right needle. Drop the main yarn and pick up the contrast yarn, taking it over the top of the dropped yarn.

3. Using the contrast yarn, knit to the position for the next color change. Spread out stitches on your right needle. Drop the contrast yarn and pick up the main yarn, taking it under the contrast yarn.

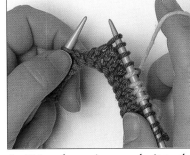

4. Using the main yarn, knit to the position for the next color change. Spread out these stitches on your right needle. Drop this yarn and pick up the contrast yarn, taking it over the top of the dropped yarn.

5. Repeat steps 3–4 across the row.

6. Turn your work. Before beginning the next row, twist the yarns once.

Hints

To ensure your work does not become puckered, always spread out the stitches you have worked since your last color change before beginning with a new color. The yarn not in use should be carried loosely on the back of the fabric.

Take care to ensure that the carried yarns do not become twisted. Always take the same color over and the same color under when making the color changes.

knitting with multiple colors and then there's more

Stranding on a Purl Row: Holding One Yarn at a Time

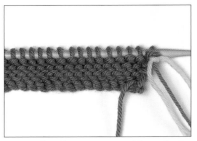

1. With the wrong side of the fabric facing you, join the contrast color at the beginning of the row.

2. Drop the contrast yarn and purl to the position for the color change. Spread out the stitches on your right needle. Drop the main yarn and pick up the contrast yarn, taking it over the top of the dropped yarn.

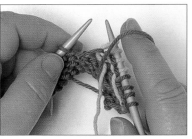

3. Using the contrast yarn, purl to the position for the next color change. Spread out these stitches on your right needle. Drop the contrast yarn and pick up the main yarn, taking it under the contrast yarn.

4. Using the main yarn, knit to the position for the next color change. Spread out these stitches on your right needle. Drop this yarn and pick up the contrast yarn, taking it over the top of the dropped yarn.

5. Repeat steps 3–4 across the row.

6. Turn your work. Before beginning the next row, twist the yarns once.

Stranding on a Knit Row: Holding Yarns with Both Hands

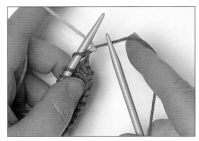

1. With the right side of the fabric facing you, join the contrast yarn at the beginning of the row. Hold the main yarn with your right hand and the contrast yarn with your left.

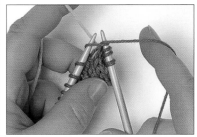

2. Knit to the position for the color change using the main yarn in your right hand and the English method (see page 26).

3. Spread out the stitches on your right needle. Using the contrast yarn in your left hand and the Continental method (see page 27), knit to the position for the next color change.

and then there's more knitting with multiple colors

Stranding on a Purl Row: Holding Yarns with Both Hands

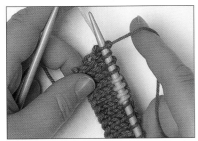

4. Spread out these stitches on your right needle. Using the main yarn in your right hand and the English method (see page 26), knit to the position for the next color change.

5. Repeat steps 3–4 across the row.

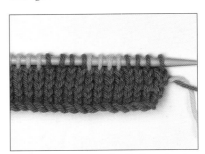

6. Turn your work. Before beginning the next row, twist the yarns once.

1. With the wrong side of the fabric facing you, join the contrast yarn at the beginning of the row. Hold the main yarn with your right hand and the contrast yarn over the thumb of your left hand.

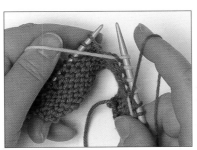

3. Spread out the stitches on your right needle. Using the contrast yarn in your left hand and the Continental method (see page 29), purl to the position for the next color change.

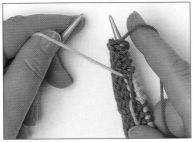

5. Repeat steps 3–4 across the row.

2. Purl to the position for the color change using the main yarn in your right hand and the English method (see page 28). Hold the contrast yarn away from the tips of the needles.

4. Spread out these stitches on your right needle. Using the main yarn in your right hand and the English method (see page 28), purl to the position for the next color change.

6. Turn your work. Before beginning the next row, twist the yarns once.

knitting with multiple colors and then there's more

97

Weaving

Use weaving when you need to carry the yarn across more than four stitches.

Weaving on a Knit Row

1. With the right side of the fabric facing you, join the contrast color at the beginning of the row.

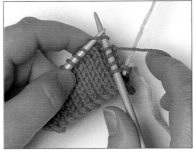

2. Knit three to four stitches with the main color, holding the contrast yarn out of the way. Spread out the stitches on your right needle. Insert the tip of your right needle into the next stitch as for a knit stitch.

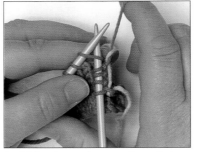

3. Take the main yarn from left to right over and around the contrast yarn (counterclockwise).

4. Wrap the main yarn around the tip of your right needle as you would for a knit stitch.

5. Complete the stitch.

6. Insert the tip of your right needle into the next stitch as for a knit stitch. Take the main yarn from left to right under and around the contrast yarn (clockwise).

Hints

To prevent a ridge from forming in your work, stagger the position you catch the carried yarn from row to row.

Weave in on every third to fourth stitch. If you do it on every alternate stitch you are likely to distort your knitted fabric.

7. Wrap the main yarn around the tip of your right needle as you would for a knit stitch.

8. Complete the stitch.

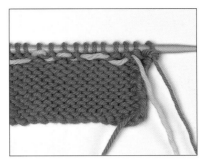

9. Repeat steps 2–8, weaving the contrast color over and under on the back, until you are ready to change color.

Weaving on a Purl Row

1. With the wrong side of the fabric facing you, join the contrast color at the beginning of the row.

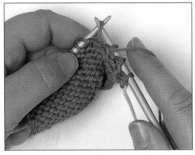

2. Purl three to four stitches with the main color, holding the contrast yarn out of the way. Spread out the stitches on your right needle. Insert the tip of your right needle into the next stitch as for a purl stitch.

3. Take the main yarn from left to right under and around the contrast yarn (counterclockwise).

4. Wrap the main yarn around the tip of your right needle as you would for a purl stitch.

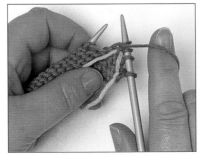

5. Complete the stitch.

6. Insert the tip of your right needle into the next stitch as for a purl stitch. Take the main yarn from left to right over and around the contrast yarn (clockwise).

knitting with multiple colors and then there's more

99

7. Wrap the main yarn around the tip of your right needle as you would for a purl stitch.

8. Complete the stitch.

9. Repeat steps 2–8, weaving the contrast color over and under on the front, until you are ready to change color.

Intarsia Knitting
In this type of knitting, the different colored yarns are not carried across a row on the back of the knitted fabric. It is great for creating large multicolored designs and pictures.

Preparing the Yarn

A separate ball of yarn is needed for each area of color across a row, and taking the time to prepare your yarns will make a huge difference to enjoying intarsia knitting. Without proper preparation you will spend more time untangling different colored yarns than you will actually knitting your garment.

1. For large areas of color, such as backgrounds, place the ball of yarn into a plastic bag. Ensure the end of the yarn hangs out of the bag and loosely secure the top with a rubber band.

2. For medium-sized areas of color, wind the yarn onto bobbins. Bobbins can be purchased or cut your own from cardboard or template plastic.

3. For very small areas, simply cut a length of yarn. To work out how much you need, wind the yarn around your needle the same number of times as the number of stitches you will need to work. Add extra for securing the ends, and cut.

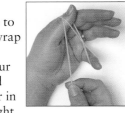

4A. As an alternative to bobbins, wrap the yarn around your thumb and little finger in a figure eight.

4B. When you have wound enough yarn, remove it from your fingers and cut the end. Wind the end around the middle a couple of times and secure with a knot.

4C. Remove the yarn from the bundle by pulling on the unknotted end.

and then there's more knitting with multiple colors

Changing Colors
Every time you change color the two yarns must be twisted together so that holes do not form in your work. Join in a new yarn following the instructions for joining in a new yarn in the middle of a row on page 37.

Changing Color Vertically on a Knit Row

1. Knit to the position for the color change. Insert your right needle into the next stitch on your left needle knitwise.

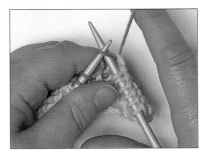

2. Drop the old color and pick up the new color from behind the old color.

When changing colors vertically, ensure the yarns are twisted at the changeover points in every row.

3. Wrap the new color from back to front around the tip of your right needle.

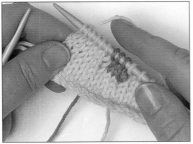

4. Complete the knit stitch. Knit to the end of the row or to the position for the next color change.

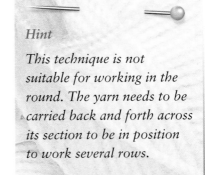

Hint

This technique is not suitable for working in the round. The yarn needs to be carried back and forth across its section to be in position to work several rows.

Changing Color Vertically on a Purl Row

1. Purl to the position for the color change. Insert your right needle into the next stitch on your left needle purlwise.

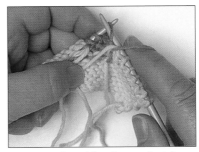

2. Drop the old color and pick up the new color, taking it under the old color.

3. Wrap the new color around the tip of your right needle in a counterclockwise direction.

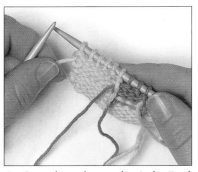

4. Complete the purl stitch. Purl to the end of the row or to the position for the next color change.

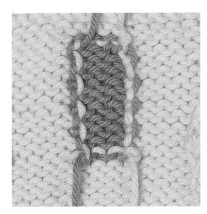

Changing Color Diagonally to the Left on a Knit Row

1. Knit to the position for the color change. Insert your right needle into the next stitch on your left needle knitwise.

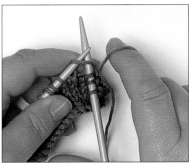

2. Drop the old color and pick up the new color, taking it under the old color.

3. Wrap the new color from back to front around the tip of your right needle.

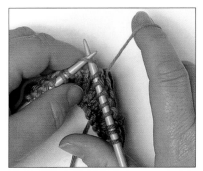

4. Complete the knit stitch. Knit to the end of the row or to the position for the next color change.

and then there's more knitting with multiple colors

Changing Color Diagonally to the Right on a Knit Row

1. Knit to the position for the color change. Insert your right needle into the next stitch on your left needle knitwise.

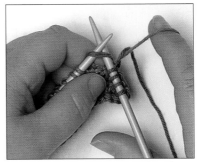

2. Drop the old color and pick up the new color, taking it under the old color.

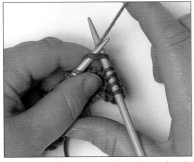

3. Wrap the new color from back to front around the tip of your right needle.

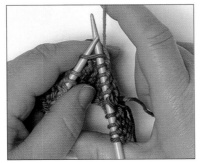

4. Complete the knit stitch. Knit to the end of the row or to the position for the next color change.

Hints

Keep the lengths of yarn unraveled from your bobbins as short as possible to help prevent them from tangling.

Always place your right needle into the next stitch before crossing the two yarns.

Changing Color Diagonally to the Left on a Purl Row

1. Purl to the position for the color change. Insert your right needle into the next stitch on your left needle purlwise.

2. Drop the old color and pick up the new color, taking it under the old color.

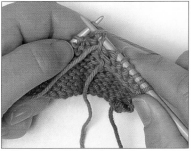

3. Wrap the new color around the tip of your right needle in a counterclockwise direction. Ensure the old color lies loosely across the stitches.

4. Complete the purl stitch. Purl to the end of the row or to the position for the next color change.

Changing Color Diagonally to the Right on a Purl Row

1. Purl to the position for the color change. Insert your right needle into the next stitch on your left needle purlwise.

2. Drop the old color and pick up the new color, taking it under the old color.

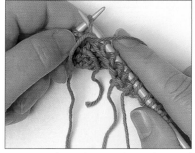

3. Wrap the new color around the tip of your right needle in a counterclockwise direction. Ensure the old color lies loosely across the stitches.

4. Complete the purl stitch. Purl to the end of the row or to the position for the next color change.

and then there's more knitting with multiple colors

Tidying the Ends of Yarn

When areas of color are completed, cut the yarn, leaving a tail 4 to 6" (10 to 15 cm) long. Ensure that all tails of yarn are left on the wrong side of the knitted fabric.

1. Thread the tail into a tapestry needle. Take the needle through the top loop of the next stitch in a different color.

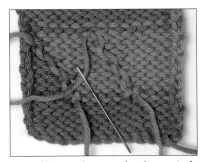

2. Pull gently until the stitch that belongs to the tail of yarn is the same tension as all the other stitches.

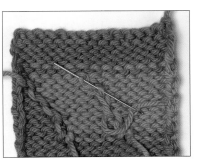

3. Weave the yarn back and forth along the edge of the shape.

4. Stretch the knitting slightly and cut off any excess yarn.

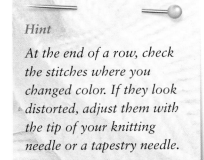

Hint

At the end of a row, check the stitches where you changed color. If they look distorted, adjust them with the tip of your knitting needle or a tapestry needle.

Embossing
Embossing can be worked across an entire row or just a small section.

Embossing in Stockinette Stitch

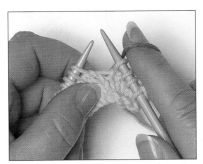

1. Work to the position for the embossing, ensuring you have the right side of the knitted fabric facing you. Join in the embossing yarn (see page 37).

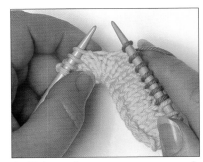

2. Using the new yarn, work knit stitches for the width of the embossed section.

3. Turn your work. Continue working stockinette stitch (alternate rows of purl and knit stitch) across the embossed section only, finishing on the wrong side. We have worked six rows.

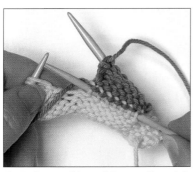

4. Using a thin cable needle, pick up the last row of stitches below the embossing.

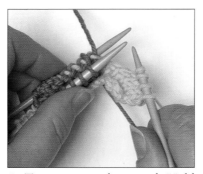

5. Turn your work around. Hold the cable needle behind your left needle.

6. Insert your right needle from left to right into the front of the first stitch on the front needle and from right to left into the back of the first stitch on the back (cable) needle.

7. Using the main yarn, knit the two stitches together.

8. Repeat steps 6–7 across all the embossed stitches.

Hint

If you are working embossed sections close together, carry the yarn on the back of the fabric in the same manner as you would for multicolored knitting.

9. If you have only worked a small section of embossing, continue knitting to the end of the row.

Embossing in stockinette stitch

Embossing in reverse stockinette stitch

and then there's more embossing

Embossing in Reverse Stockinette Stitch

With this method the embossed sections are beautifully rounded.

1. Work to the position for the embossing, ensuring you have the right side of the knitted fabric facing you. Join in the embossing yarn (see page 37).

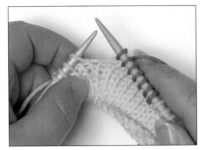

2. Using the new yarn, work knit stitches for the width of the embossed section.

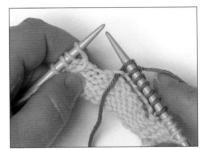

3. Turn your work. Work a second row of knit stitch across the embossed section only.

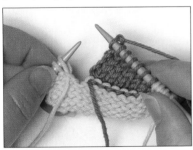

4. Turn your work. Work the next row with purl stitch and then alternate between knit and purl rows for the desired number of rows, finishing on the wrong side. We have worked six rows.

5. Using a thin cable needle, pick up the last row of stitches below the embossing.

6. Turn your work around. Hold the cable needle behind your left needle.

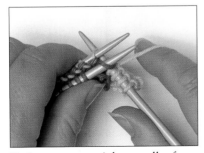

7. Insert your right needle from left to right into the front of the first stitch on the front needle and from right to left into the back of the first stitch on the back (cable) needle.

8. Using the main yarn, knit the two stitches together.

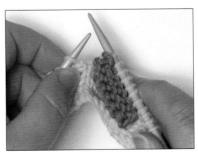

9. Repeat steps 7–8 across all the embossed stitches. If you have only worked a small section of embossing, continue knitting to the end of the row.

This
fascinating
technique
creates a
knitted fabric
reminiscent
of patchwork
or weaving.

Entrelac Knitting

Base Triangles
In our example we have used eight stitches for each triangle. Any number can be used as long as you keep it the same for each triangle and block. Each shape will be made from approximately twice as many rows as the number of stitches used.

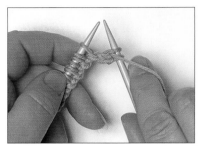

1. Cast on the required number of stitches (our sample is a multiple of eight). Purl the first two stitches.

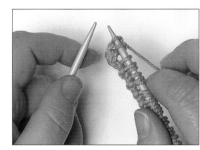

2. Turn your work and knit the same two stitches you just purled.

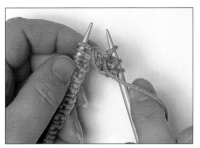

3. Turn your work and purl the same two stitches and then one stitch extra.

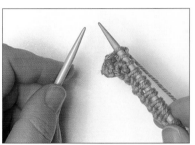

4. Turn your work and knit the same three stitches.

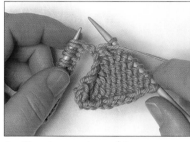

5. Continue in this manner, adding an extra stitch in each purl row until you have eight stitches on your right needle. The last row is a purl row.

6. Without turning your work, purl the next two stitches.

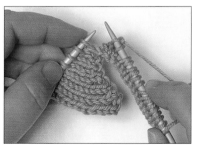

7. Turn your work and knit the same two stitches you just purled.

8. Turn and purl three. Turn, knit three. Continue in this manner, adding an extra stitch in each purl row until you have eight stitches on your right needle. The last row is a purl row.

9. Repeat steps 6–8 until the required number of base triangles is worked.

First Row of Blocks

The first row of blocks begins and ends with side triangles.

1. Starting side triangle. Change yarn color. Knit two stitches. Turn and purl the same two stitches.

2. Turn. Knit the first stitch but do not drop it from your left needle.

3. Insert your right needle from left to right into the back of the stitch still remaining on your left needle.

4. Complete the stitch, dropping it from your left needle.

5. Slip the next stitch on your left needle onto your right needle knitwise.

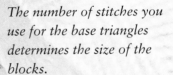

6. Knit the next stitch (this stitch is from the base triangle).

7. Pick up the slipped stitch with your left needle and pass it over the last stitch.

entrelac knitting and then there's more

8. Turn your work and purl three.

9. Turn. Knit into the front and then the back of the first stitch following steps 2–4.

10. Knit up to the last stitch in the second yarn color. Slip this last stitch onto your right needle knitwise.

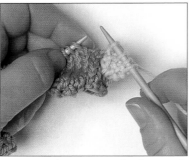

11. Knit the next stitch (this stitch is from the base triangle). Pick up the slipped stitch with your left needle and pass it over the last stitch.

12. Turn your work and purl across the row.

13. Repeat steps 9–12 until only one stitch from the base triangle remains on your left needle. Turn your work and purl across the row.

14. Turn your work and repeat steps 9–11. No stitches from the base triangle remain on your needle.

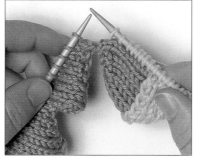

15. First block. Pick up and knit eight stitches along the adjacent side of the base triangle (see page 50).

16. Turn your work and purl eight.

and then there's more entrelac knitting

17. Turn. Knit up to the last stitch in the second yarn.

18. Slip the next stitch on your left needle onto your right needle knit-wise. Knit next stitch. Pick up the slipped stitch with your left needle and pass it over the last stitch.

19. Repeat steps 17 and 18 until all stitches of the second base triangle are off the needle.

20. Second and remaining blocks. Pick up eight stitches along the adjacent side of the base triangle and work a second block following steps 15–19. Repeat for all the blocks along the row.

21. Finishing side triangle. Pick up and knit eight stitches along the adjacent side of the last base triangle.

22. Turn your work and purl the first two stitches together.

23. Purl the remaining six picked up stitches.

24. Turn and knit seven.

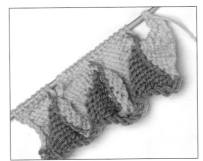

25. Turn, purl two together, and purl five. Turn and knit six. Turn, purl two together and purl four. Turn and knit five. Continue decreasing in this manner until one stitch remains. Slip this last stitch back onto your left needle.

entrelac knitting and then there's more

Second Row of Blocks
The second row of blocks does not have any side triangles.

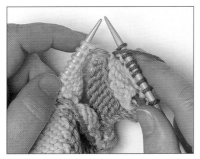

1. First block. Change yarn color. Purl one stitch. Pick up and purl seven stitches along the edge of the side triangle.

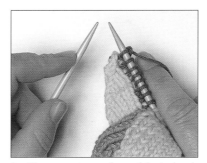

2. Turn your work and knit back across the eight stitches.

3. Turn. Purl to the last stitch in the new yarn color. Purl two stitches together (the last stitch in the new yarn and the first stitch in the old yarn).

4. Repeat steps 2–3 until all the stitches of the block in the first row of blocks are off the needles.

5. Work all the blocks across the row in the same manner, picking up eight stitches for each new block.

Subsequent Rows of Blocks

Continue working rows of blocks alternating between the first and second rows of blocks. Finish with a first row of blocks.

Finishing Triangles

1. Change yarn color. Purl one stitch. Pick up and purl seven stitches along the edge of the side triangle.

2. Turn your work and knit back across the stitches.

3. Turn. Purl two stitches together, purl to the last stitch in the new yarn color, and purl two stitches together (the last stitch in the new yarn and the first stitch in the old yarn).

and then there's more entrelac knitting

4. Repeat steps 2–3 until only two stitches in the new yarn remain on the needle. Turn and knit two.

5. Turn, purl one, and then purl two together.

6. Turn and knit two.

7. Turn and purl three together. One stitch remains on your right needle.

8. Pick up and purl seven stitches along the edge of the next block.

9. Repeat steps 2–7 to form a second triangle.

10. Continue working triangles across the entire row in the same manner.

Lace Knitting

Lace knitting is also known as openwork. Each pattern is a balance between increases, to create holes in the knitted fabric, and decreases, to maintain the shape of the overall piece. Yarnovers are the most commonly used increases because these create the best holes! See pages 39–47 for step-by-step instructions for forming increases and decreases.

Positions of Yarn for Yarn Overs

Yarn over between two knit stitches

Yarn over between two purl stitches

Yarn over after a knit stitch and before a purl stitch

Yarn over after a purl stitch and before a knit stitch

Multiple Yarn Overs

Multiple yarn overs can be used to create large holes. The additional yarn overs are often dropped in the next row so that the knitting has only increased by one stitch. No matter how the first yarn over is formed, all subsequent ones are formed in the same way.

Position of yarn for two yarn overs

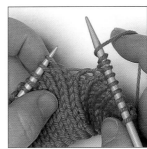

Position of yarn for three yarn overs

Loop Knitting
Loop knitting can be used to create a mock fur effect. You can use it for a complete garment or just for items such as collars and cuffs.

Single Loop Method

Hints

Avoid working loops in seam allowances because they will just get in the way.

Don't use loop knitting on items for babies and small children. Little fingers can be easily tangled in the loops.

To keep the loops all on the same side of the knitted fabric, only work them in every alternate row.

Adjust the density of your loops by working them on every stitch or every alternate stitch across a row.

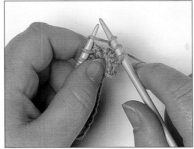

1. On the right side of the fabric, knit to the position for the first loop. Knit the next stitch but do not drop it from your left needle.

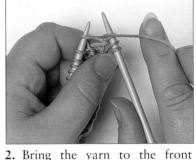

2. Bring the yarn to the front between the two needles.

3. Take the yarn around your left thumb in a clockwise direction and then take it to the back between the two needles.

4. Insert your right needle from left to right into the front of the first stitch on your left needle (this is the stitch you already knitted into before making a loop around your thumb).

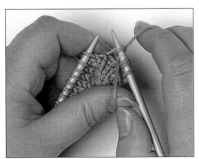

5. Finish knitting the stitch, slipping it onto your right needle.

6. Slip the first two stitches on your right needle back onto your left needle.

7. Insert your right needle from right to left into the back of both stitches on your left needle.

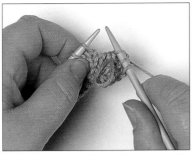

8. Complete the knit stitch, knitting both stitches together. You now have the same number of stitches that you started with.

9. Repeat steps 1–8 across the row for the desired number of loops.

10. Turn your work and stitch across the wrong side without forming any loops.

11. Work the next row and every alternate row with the desired number of loops.

12. When the knitting is finished, the loops can be cut or left uncut.

Cluster Loop Method

This method produces denser loops than the single loop method but the loops cannot be cut.

1. On the wrong side of the fabric, purl to the position for the first loop. Take the yarn to the back between the needles.

2. Insert your right needle from left to right into the front of the next stitch on your left needle.

3. Depending on the size of the loops you want, place one to two fingers from your left hand behind your right needle.

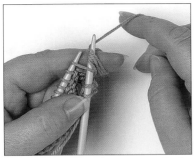

4. Winding clockwise, wind the yarn around the tip of your right needle and your fingers three times. Finish with the yarn just over the tip of the needle.

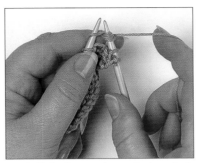

5. Pull the loops through the stitch on your left needle with your right needle. Do not drop the stitch or the loops off your needles.

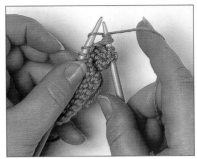

6. Remove your fingers from the loops.

7. Slip the loops onto your left needle.

8. Insert your right needle from right to left into the back of all three loops and the original stitch on your left needle.

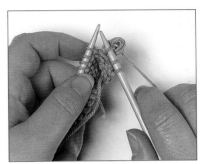

9. Knit all the loops together.

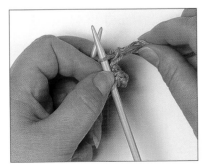

10. On the right side of the knitted fabric, pull the loops firmly to lock them in position.

11. Repeat steps 1–9 across the row for the desired number of loops.

12. Turn your work and stitch across the right side without forming any loops.

loop knitting and then there's more

13. Work the next row and every alternate row with the desired number of loops.

Shaker Knitting

Shaker knitting is also known as fisherman's rib and is created by using yarn overs. A shaker-knitted garment will use 30% to 50% more yarn than the same garment worked in stockinette stitch.

Double Shaker Knitting

Double shaker knitting looks the same on both sides of the knitted fabric.

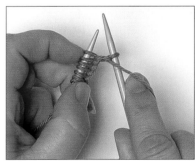

1. Cast on an odd number of stitches. **Row 1.** Tightly purl the first stitch for the selvage.

2. Knit the next stitch.

3. Bring the yarn to the front between the tips of your needles. Insert the tip of your right needle from right to left into the front of the next stitch on your left needle.

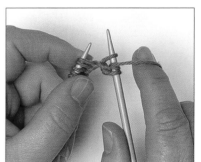

4. Slip the stitch onto your right needle.

and then there's more loop knitting shaker knitting

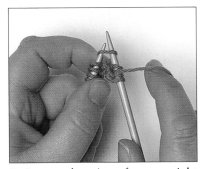

5. Insert the tip of your right needle from left to right into the front of the next stitch on your left needle in preparation for knitting this stitch.

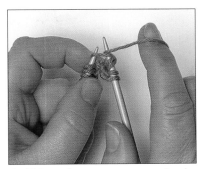

6. Take the yarn around the tip of your right needle in a counterclockwise direction.

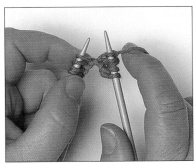

7. Finish knitting the stitch, slipping it onto your right needle.

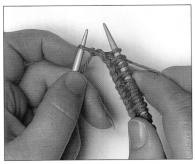

8. Repeat steps 3–7 across the row until reaching the last stitch.

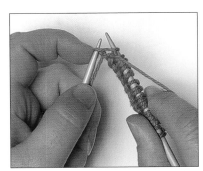

9. Tightly purl this last stitch for the selvage.

10. Row 2. Turn your work. Tightly purl the first stitch for the selvage.

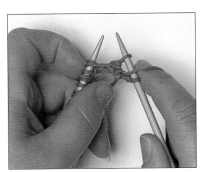

11. With the yarn at the front, slip the next stitch onto your right needle purlwise.

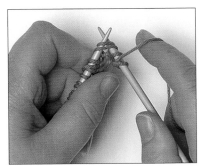

12. Insert your right needle from left to right behind both the yarn over and next stitch on your left needle.

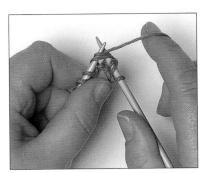

13. Take the yarn around the tip of your right needle in a counterclockwise direction.

shaker knitting and then there's more

119

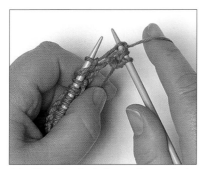

14. Finish knitting the stitch, slipping it onto your right needle.

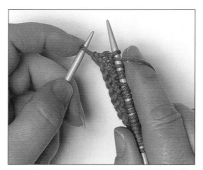

15. Repeat steps 11–14 across the row, finishing with step 11.

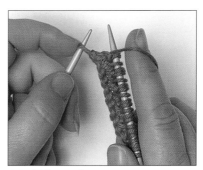

16. Take the yarn counter-clockwise around your right needle, finishing at the front, to form a yarn over.

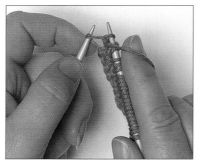

17. Tightly purl the last stitch for the selvage.

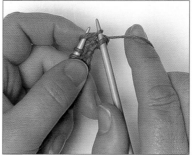

18. Row 3. Turn your work. Tightly purl the first stitch for the selvage. Starting with the yarn at the back, knit the next stitch and yarn over together.

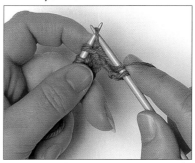

19. Bring the yarn to the front and slip the next stitch onto your right needle purlwise.

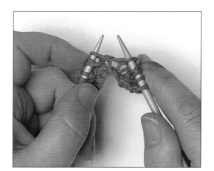

20. Knit the next stitch and yarn over together.

21. Repeat steps 19–20 across the row to the last stitch. Tightly purl this last stitch for the selvage.

22. Continue, alternating rows 2 and 3, until your work is the desired length.

and then there's more shaker knitting

Single Shaker Knitting
The stitches on one side of the knitted fabric will appear smooth, much like the texture achieved with double shaker knitting, and the stitches on the other side will appear a little uneven. Either can be used as the right side of the fabric.

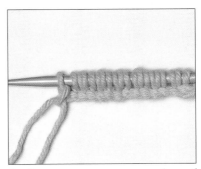

1. Cast on an uneven number of stitches. **Row 1.** Work row 1 following steps 1–9 on pages 118–119.

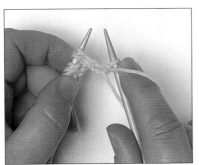

2. Row 2. Turn your work. Tightly purl the first stitch of the second row for the selvage.

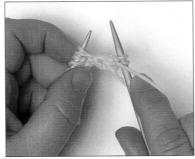

3. Purl the next stitch.

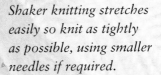

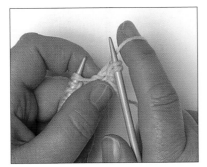

4. Take the yarn to the back between the tips of the needles.

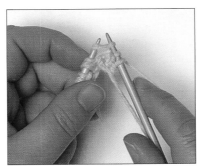

5. Knit the next stitch and yarn over together.

Hints

Shaker knitting stretches easily so knit as tightly as possible, using smaller needles if required.

Because shaker knitting uses a lot of yarn, select a lightweight yarn. Your garment will be less likely to stretch and be more comfortable to wear.

Double shaker knitting has a tendency to stretch across the width and single shaker knitting is more likely to stretch down the length.

shaker knitting and then there's more

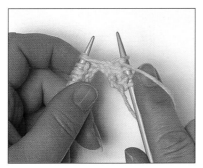

6. Bring the yarn to the front between the tips of the needles. Purl the next stitch.

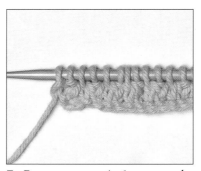

7. Repeat steps 4–6 across the row until the last stitch. Tightly purl this last stitch for the selvage.

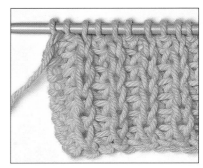

8. Continue, alternating rows 1 and 2, until your work is the desired length.

Surface Embroidery on Knitting

Threads and Needles to Use

The huge array of embroidery threads and yarns available to you can be confusing or exciting. Choose ones that have care requirements that complement your knitted garment. Very fine threads will sink into your knitting and be obscured. Threads that are chunkier than your knitting may distort it.

Tapestry needles are an excellent choice. Their blunt tips mean that you are less likely to split the yarn of the knitted stitches. However, if you are also stitching through a layer of organza or the like, use a needle with a sharp point.

Anchoring Threads

To anchor your embroidery thread at the beginning of your design use a waste knot. Knot the end of the thread. This knot does not have to be dainty or neat. In fact, a bit of bulk will help it stay in place. It will be removed before you have finished your garment. Place the waste knot on the right side of the knitting approximately 3" (7.5 cm) away from where you will start stitching and then bring the thread to the front at your starting position.

To end off tails of thread, simply weave them back and forth behind the embroidery on the back of the knitted fabric. Snip off the waste knots and weave these tails of thread in the same manner.

Waste knots and embroidery

Woven tails on back of embroidery

Stabilizing the Surface and Transferring Designs

The elastic and sometimes chunky nature of knitting, compared to woven fabrics, can make it difficult to successfully embroider directly onto it.

Lightweight knitted fabric can be permanently backed with a lightweight, nonfusible interfacing. To do this, cut a piece of interfacing slightly larger than the embroidery design. Position it on the back of the knitted fabric behind the section to be embroidered. Baste the interfacing to the knitted fabric and then embroider through both the knitted fabric and the interfacing. When the embroidery is complete, cut away the excess interfacing (see below).

The following method and materials allow you to both transfer your embroidery design and stabilize the knitted fabric while stitching onto it. Cut a piece of waste canvas; lightweight, nonfusible, woven interfacing; organza; or tracing paper at least 1" (2.5 cm) larger than your embroidery design. Place this over the embroidery design and trace it with a graphite pencil or fabric marker. If it is difficult to see the design through the material, place it over a window or light box. The light shining through will make it easier to see.

Cutting away interfacing on back of knitting from behind embroidery

Basting with running stitch

Basting with whipstitch

Position the tracing onto the right side of your knitted fabric, ensuring it is positioned how you would like. Baste the two fabrics together using either a running stitch or a whipstitch (fabric is less likely to fray and pull out of shape with whipstitch).

Embroider through both the tracing and the knitted fabric. When the embroidery is finished, remove the tracing. If you have used a fabric such as waste canvas, woven interfacing, or organza, remove it strand by strand. Tweezers are a real boon in helping you do this.

Removing traced fabric with tweezers

Maintaining Elasticity

Embroidery stitches are most often worked on woven fabrics and like these fabrics, they have no elasticity. Working these stitches on a stretchy fabric such as knitting will inhibit this stretchiness.

Here are some ways to minimize this problem:

- Work with an even tension but take care not to pull stitches too tightly.

- Because knitting stretches sideways rather than up and down, vertical (as opposed to horizontal) embroidery designs will have less of an impact on the stretchiness of the finished garment.

- If carrying threads on the back of knitted fabrics, only do so for short distances.

- Use only small or open embroidery designs. If a design requires a large area to be covered with one color, consider knitting this into the garment rather than embroidering it.

- Avoid or take particular care with areas that need to stretch, such as neck and sleeve bands.

- Don't be tempted to use overlong horizontal stitches. As well as inhibiting elasticity, they are more likely to catch than shorter stitches.

Blanket Stitch
This stitch can be used to reinforce buttonholes and other edges as well as being decorative. The height and width of the stitches can be varied to create the look you want.

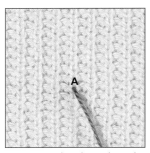

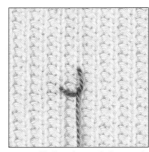

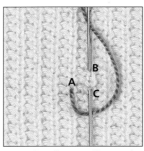

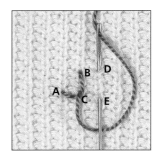

1. Bring the thread to the front at A. This is the base of the first blanket stitch on the left-hand side.

2. Take the needle to the back at B and re-emerge at C. Ensure the thread is under the tip of the needle.

3. Pull the thread through until it lies snugly against the emerging thread but does not distort the fabric.

4. Take the needle to the back at D and re-emerge at E. Ensure the thread lies under the tip of the needle.

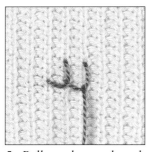

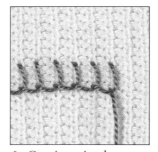

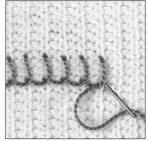

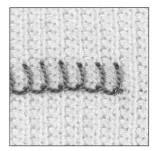

5. Pull the thread through as before.

6. Continue in the same manner.

7. To finish, take the needle to the back of the fabric just over the last loop.

8. Pull the thread through and fasten off on the back of the fabric.

Cross Stitch: Individual

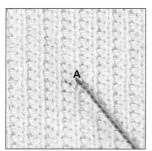

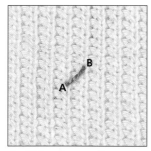

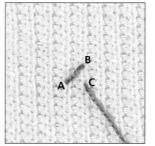

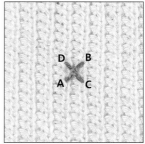

1. Secure the thread on the back of the fabric and bring it to the front at A.

2. Take the needle to the back at B, above and to the right of A. Pull the thread through.

3. Bring the thread to the front at C, directly below B. Pull the thread through.

4. Take the needle to the back at D, directly above A. Pull the thread through and fasten off on the back of the fabric.

Cross Stitch: In Rows

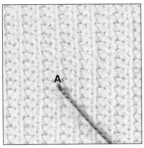

1. Secure the thread on the back of the fabric and bring it to the front at A.

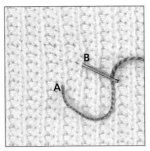

2. Take the needle to the back at B, above and to the right of A.

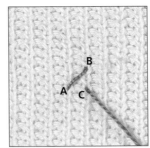

3. Pull the thread through. Bring the thread to the front at C, directly below B.

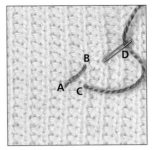

4. Take the needle to the back at D, above and to the right of C.

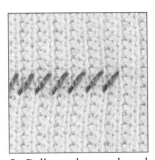

5. Pull the thread through. Continue across the row in the same manner for the required number of stitches.

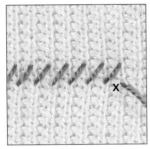

6. Bring the thread to the front at X.

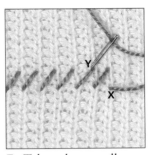

7. Take the needle to the back at Y, using the same hole in the fabric as before.

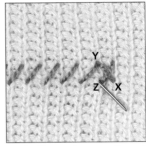

8. Pull the thread through. Re-emerge at Z, using the same hole in the fabric as before.

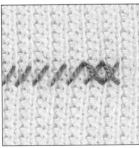

9. Pull the thread through. Work a second diagonal stitch following steps 7–8.

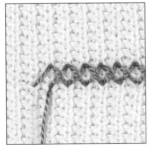

10. Continue across the row in the same manner.

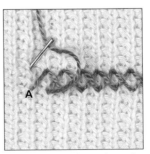

11. To finish, take the needle to the back of the fabric directly above A.

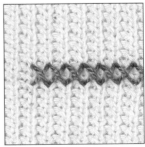

12. Pull the thread through and fasten off on the back of the fabric.

Bullion Knot ↑ Indicates top of fabric

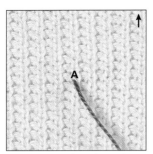

1. Secure the thread on the back of the fabric and bring it to the front at A.

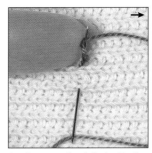

2. Take the needle to the back at B. Re-emerge at A, taking care not to split the thread.

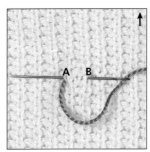

3. Rotate the fabric. Raise the tip of the needle away from the fabric. Wrap the thread clockwise around the needle.

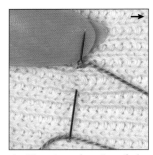

4. Keeping the tip of the needle raised, pull the wrap firmly down onto the fabric.

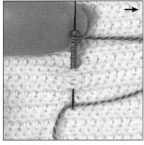

5. Work the required number of wraps around the needle. The number of wraps must cover the distance from A to B plus an extra one to two wraps. Pack them down evenly as you wrap.

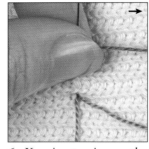

6. Keeping tension on the wraps with your thumb, begin to ease the needle through the fabric and wraps.

7. Continuing to keep tension on the wraps with your thumb, pull the thread through (thumb not shown).

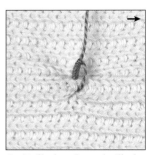

8. Pull the thread all the way through, tugging it away from you.

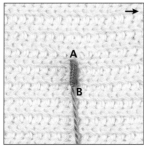

9. Release the thread. Smooth out the fabric and the knot will lie back toward B.

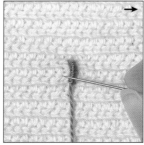

10. To ensure all the wraps are even, gently stroke and manipulate them with the needle while maintaining tension on the thread.

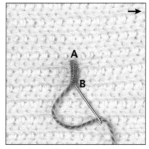

11. To finish, take the needle to the back at B.

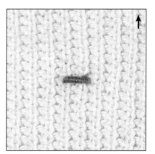

12. Pull the thread through and fasten off on the back of the fabric.

and then there's more surface embroidery on knitting

126

Couching

Couching is a particularly useful technique. Ribbons, braids, cords and ornamental threads can all be secured using the method below.

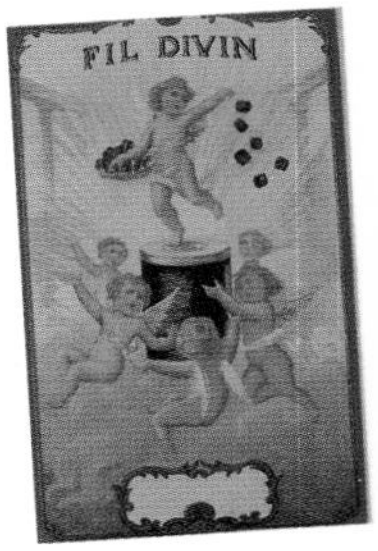

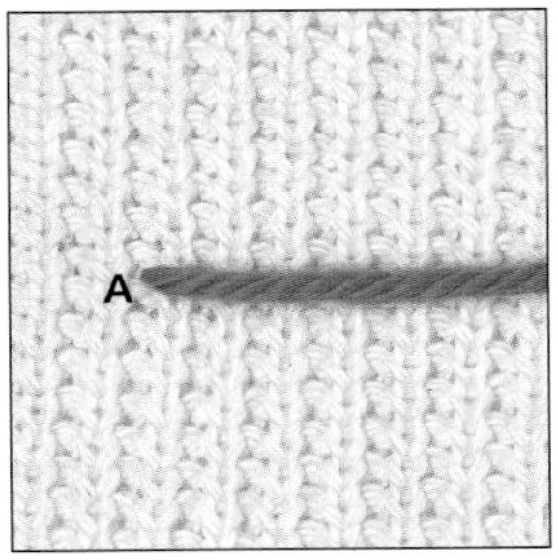

1. Secure the foundation thread on the back of the fabric and bring it to the front at A. Lay the thread on the fabric.

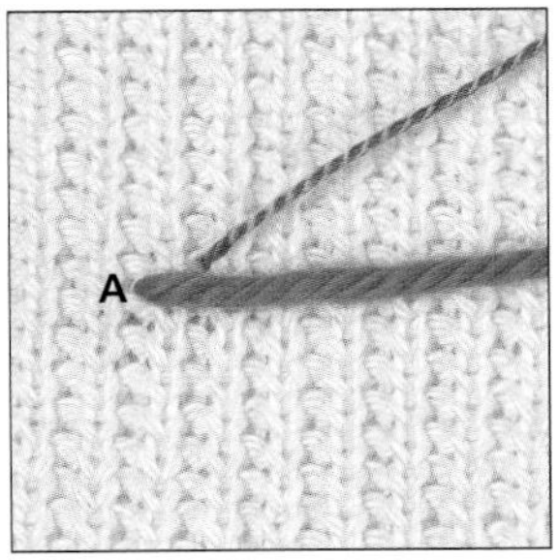

2. Bring the couching thread to the front just above the laid thread near A.

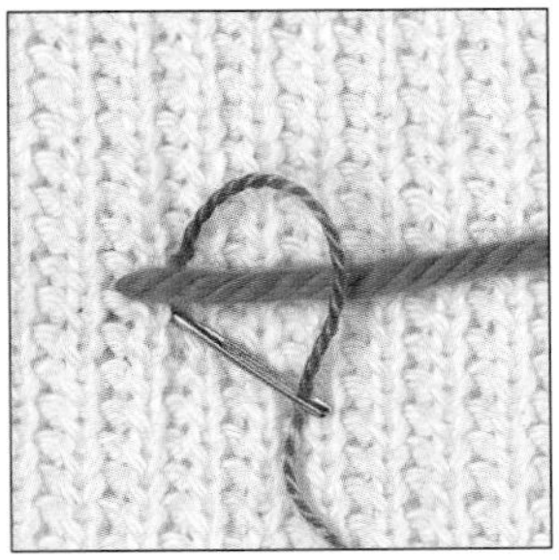

3. Take the needle over the laid thread and to the back of the fabric.

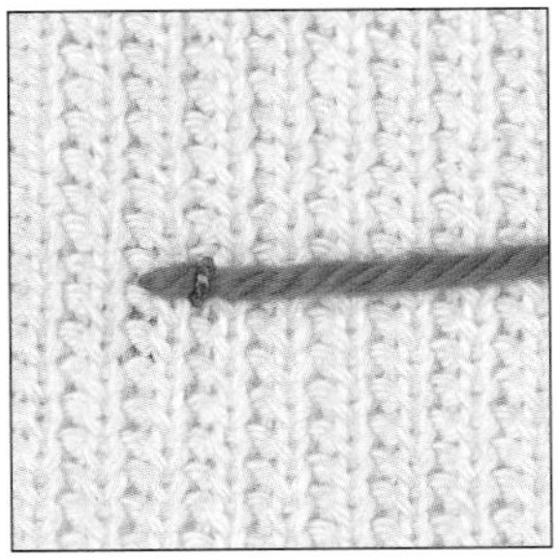

4. Pull the thread through to form the first couching stitch.

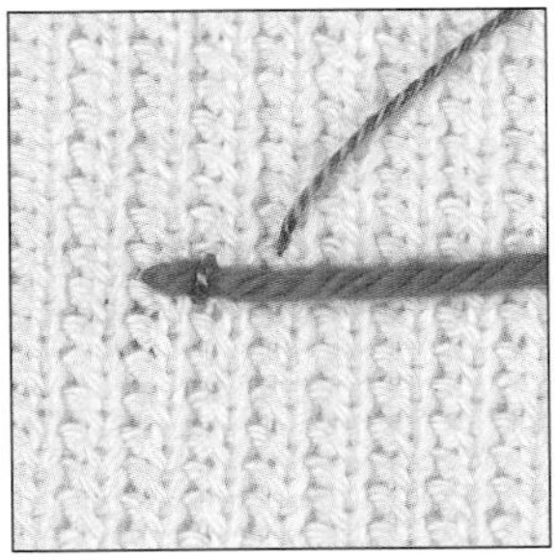

5. Bring the thread to the front just above the laid thread a short distance away.

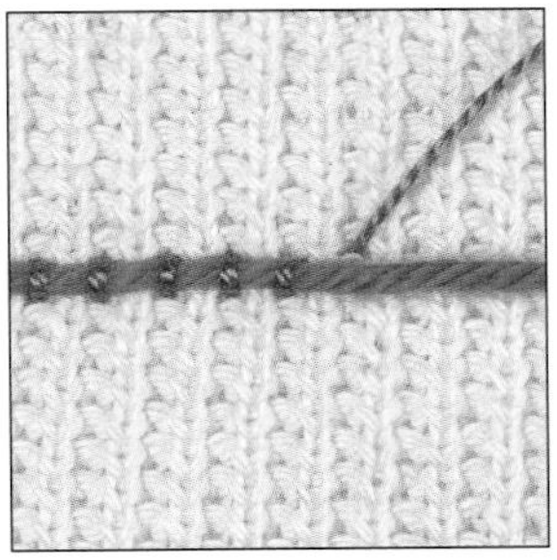

6. Continue working stitches in the same manner for the required distance.

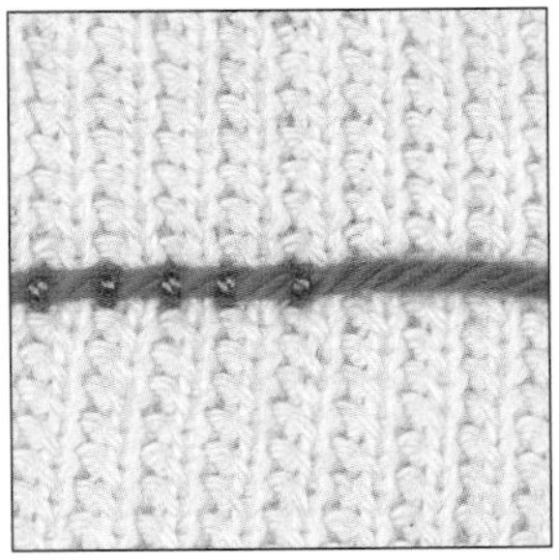

7. Take the couching thread to the back of the fabric and fasten off.

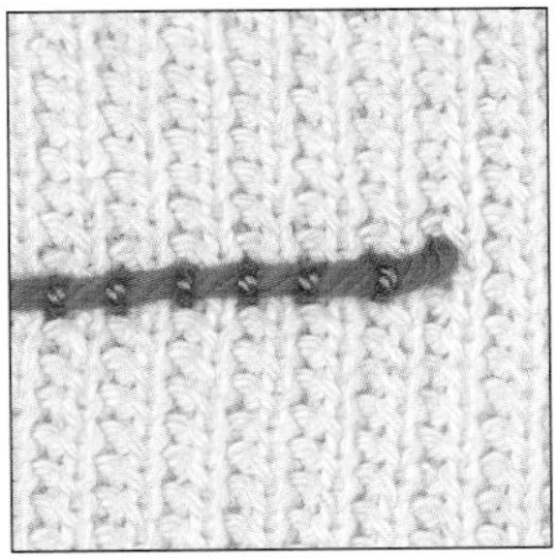

8. Take the laid thread to the back of the fabric and fasten off.

Chain Stitch

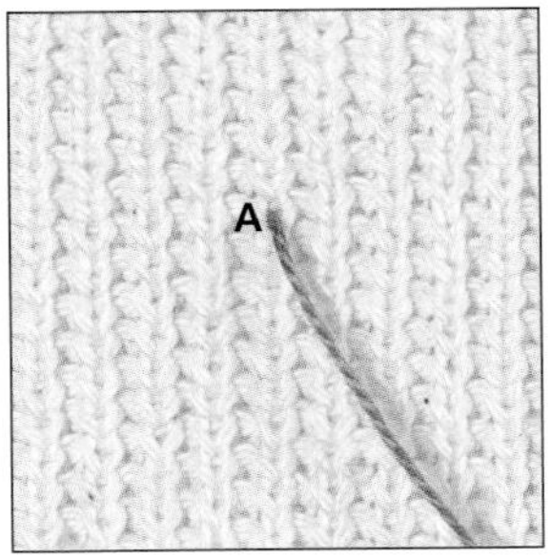

1. Secure the thread on the back of the fabric and bring it to the front at A.

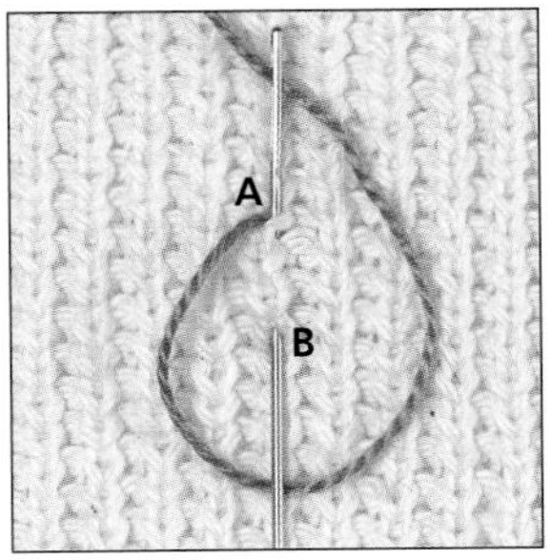

2. Take the needle from A to B, using the same hole in the fabric at A. Loop the thread under the tip of the needle.

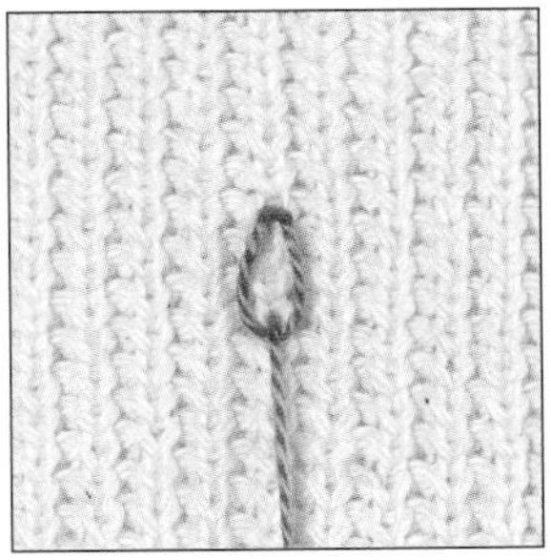

3. Pull the thread through until the loop lies snugly against the emerging thread.

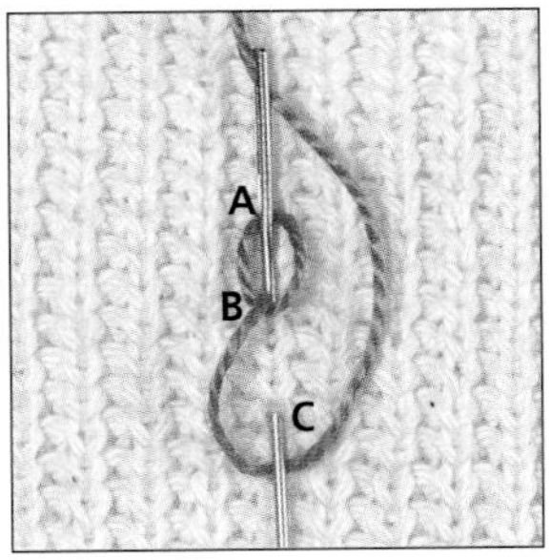

4. Take the needle through the same hole in the fabric at B and emerge at C. Loop the thread under the tip of the needle.

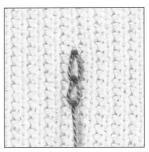

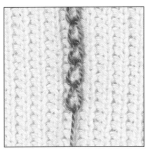

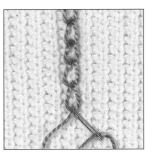

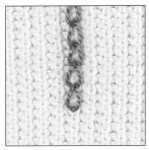

5. Pull the thread through as before.

6. Continue working chain stitches in the same manner.

7. To finish, take the needle to the back just over the last loop.

8. Pull the thread through and fasten off on the back of the fabric.

Detached Chain Detached chains are wonderful for creating simple petals and leaves.

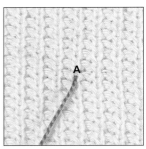

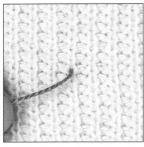

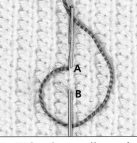

1. Bring the thread to the front at A. This is the base of the stitch.

2. Hold the thread to the left.

3. Take the needle to the back at A, through the same hole in the fabric. Emerge at B. Loop the thread under the tip of the needle.

Hint

To prevent stitches from falling into the holes of the knitting, ensure each stitch crosses the front of a knitted stitch, not just the back of a stitch. This is particularly important when working knot stitches such as bullions and French knots.

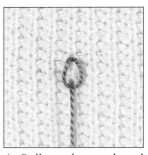

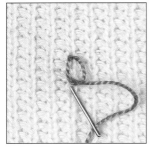

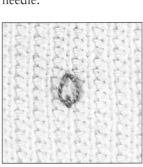

4. Pull the thread through. The tighter you pull, the thinner the stitch will become.

5. To finish, take the needle to the back just over the end of the loop.

6. Pull the thread through and fasten off on the back of the fabric.

and then there's more surface embroidery on knitting

French Knot

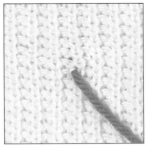

1. Bring the thread to the front at the position for the knot, splitting the yarn of the knitting.

2. Hold the thread firmly approximately 1⅛" (3 cm) from the fabric.

3. Take the thread over the needle, ensuring the needle points away from the fabric.

4. Wrap the thread around the needle. Keeping the thread taut, turn the tip of the needle towards the fabric.

5. Take the tip of the needle to the back of the fabric a short distance away, again splitting the yarn of the knitting.

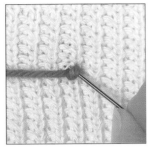

6. Slide the knot down the needle onto the fabric. Pull the thread until the knot is firmly around the needle.

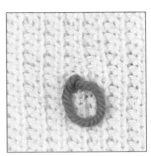

7. Push the needle through the fabric. Hold the knot in place with your thumb and pull the thread through (thumb not shown).

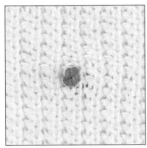

8. Pull until the loop of thread completely disappears. Fasten off on the back of the fabric.

Satin Stitch
Satin stitch has no stretch, so only use it for small areas of a design.

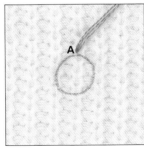

1. Secure the thread on the back of the fabric and bring it to the front at A, just outside the marked outline.

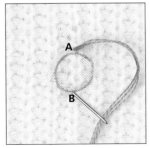

2. Take the needle to the back at B, just over the marked outline and directly opposite A.

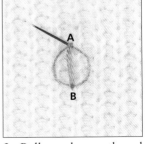

3. Pull the thread through. Emerge next to A.

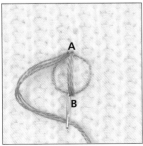

4. Pull the thread through. Take the needle to the back of the fabric next to B.

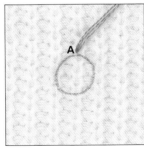

surface embroidery on knitting and then there's more

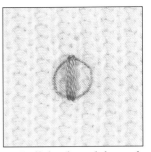

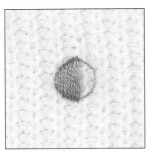

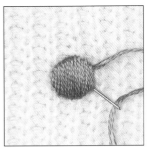

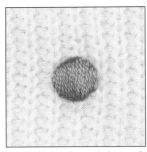

5. Pull the thread through to complete the second stitch.

6. Working in the same manner, fill one half of the shape.

7. Fill the second half in the same manner. To finish, take the needle to the back of the fabric for the last stitch.

8. Pull the thread through and fasten off on the back of the fabric.

Stem Stitch

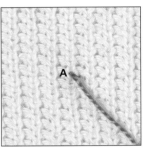

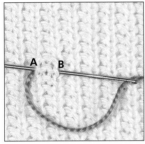

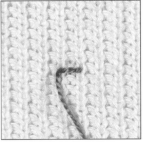

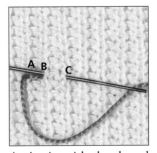

1. Bring the thread to the front at A.

2. With the thread below the needle, take the needle to the back at B and re-emerge at A.

3. Pull the thread through to complete the first stitch.

4. Again with the thread below the needle, take the needle to the back at C and emerge at B.

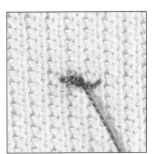

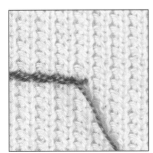

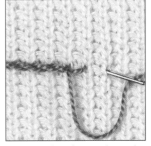

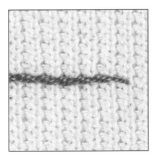

5. Pull the thread through to complete the second stitch.

6. Continue working stitches in the same manner, always keeping the thread below the needle.

7. To finish, take the needle to the back for the last stitch and do not emerge.

8. Pull the thread through and fasten off on the back of the fabric.

and then there's more surface embroidery on knitting

Duplicate Stitch

This special form of embroidery is also known as Swiss darning. It is a quick and easy way to add color and interest to your knitting. The stitches echo the shape of stockinette stitches.

Threads and Needles to Use

Use a large tapestry needle for your stitching. The blunt tip will help minimize the risk of splitting the knitting stitches.

A wide variety of threads or yarns can be used. Stranded threads and yarns approximately the same thickness as that used for the knitting are your best choice. The idea is to completely cover the stockinette stitches but not distort them.

Hints

Test your selected thread or yarn on your gauge swatch to check that it will cover the knitting stitches.

Persian yarn is excellent for duplicate stitch because it is available in a huge range of colors and can be divided into one, two, or three strands.

Begin your stitching with a waste knot 3" to 4" (8 to 10 cm) away from your starting position. See page 122.

Stitch with a loose tension. Your stitches should just rest on the knitting stitches without being loopy.

End your thread or yarn by weaving it through the back of the knitting behind the embroidery.

Horizontal Stitches: Working from Right to Left across the Fabric

1. Bring the thread to the front at the center of the base of a stockinette stitch.

2. Slide the needle from right to left behind the stockinette stitch directly above.

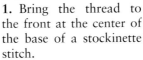

3. Pull the thread through. Take the needle back through the center of the base of the same stockinette stitch. Emerge through the center of the base of the next stockinette stitch to the left.

4. Pull the thread through.

5. Repeat steps 2–4 for the desired number of stitches.

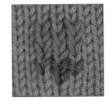 

Alternate between this step-by-step sequence and the one on the next page to fill a shape with several rows of duplicate stitch.

duplicate stitch and then there's more

Horizontal Stitches:
Working from Left to Right across the Fabric

Use this step-by-step sequence in conjunction with the one on the previous page to fill a shape with several rows of duplicate stitch.

↑ Indicates top of fabric

1. Bring the thread to the front at the center of the base of a stockinette stitch.

2. Turn the knitted fabric upside down.

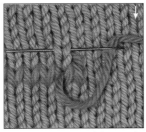

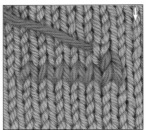

3. Slide the needle from right to left behind the stockinette stitch directly below.

4. Pull the thread through. Take needle back through center of the same stitch. Emerge through center of next stitch to the left.

5. Pull the thread through.

6. Repeat steps 3–5 for the desired number of stitches.

Vertical Stitches

1. Bring the thread to the front at the center of the base of a stockinette stitch.

2. Slide the needle from right to left behind the stockinette stitch above.

Hint

Wherever possible use the horizontal method in preference to the vertical method.

Because the horizontal method follows the path of the yarn in the knitting more accurately, it creates a neater duplicate stitch.

3. Pull the thread through. Slide needle from top to bottom behind the base of the stitch directly below.

4. Pull the thread through.

5. Repeat steps 2–4 for the desired number of stitches.

and then there's more duplicate stitch

Smocking on Knitting

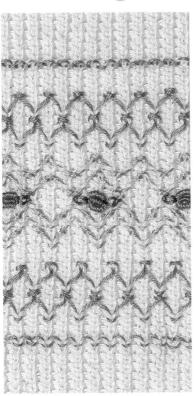

Traditional geometric smocking stitches can also be used to decorate your knitting. The two halves of a stockinette stitch represent two pleats.

Like surface embroidery, a variety of threads can be used. Try stranded and pearl cottons, blending filaments, tapestry and Persian yarns, fine cords, knitting ribbons, and even mixing different threads together. Work the smocking using a tapestry needle. The blunt end will make it less likely to split the knitting stitches.

You will also find that it is easiest to work on a background of stockinette stitch or rib stitch.

Hints

Keep your tension even but do not pull stitches too tight. They need to rest on top of the knitting stitches, not be pulled into them.

It is easier to see the smocking stitches if your knitted fabric is worked with a smooth yarn rather than a knobbly one.

Work all rows from left to right if you are right-handed and from right to left if you are left-handed.

Preparing the Knitted Fabric

1. Mark the center of the knitted fabric by tying a scrap of thread or yarn around the center top stitch. Alternatively, mark it with a small safety pin. Don't use a normal dressmaking pin, because they have a tendency to fall out!

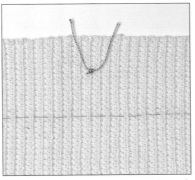

2. Using a contrasting thread, weave it along one row of knitting stitches as a guideline.

3. Repeat this procedure, at intervals, down the knitted fabric.

Smocker's Knot

A smocker's knot can be used to secure the beginnings and ends of thread.

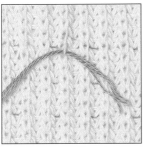

1. Take the thread through the knitting at the edge of the garment, splitting the yarn. Leave a tail of approximately 1/2" (12 mm).

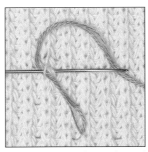

2. Keeping the thread above the needle, work a small back stitch.

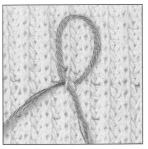

3. Pull the thread through, leaving a small loop approximately 1/2" (12 mm) long.

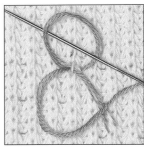

4. Take the needle through the loop.

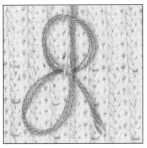

5. Pull the thread through, leaving a second loop approximately the same size as the first loop.

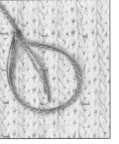

6. Holding the thread with your left hand and the second loop with your right hand, begin to pull the second loop.

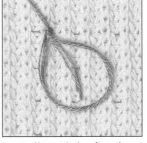

7. Pull until the first loop disappears.

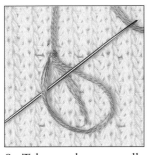

8. Take the needle through the remaining loop.

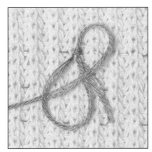

9. Begin to pull the thread through.

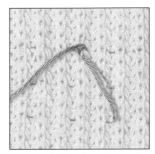

10. Pull the thread until a firm knot forms.

and then there's more smocking on knitting

Cable Stitch

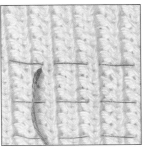

1. Secure your thread on the back of the knitted fabric. Bring it to the front on the left hand side of the first knit stitch after the seam allowance.

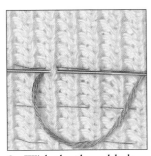

2. With the thread below the needle, take the needle from right to left behind the second half of the first knit stitch.

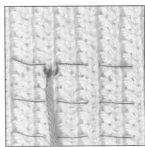

3. Pull the thread through. Tug downward gently to reposition the thread for the next stitch.

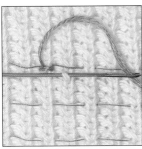

4. With the thread above the needle, take the needle from right to left behind the first half of the next knit stitch.

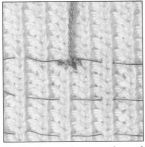

5. Pull the thread through. Tug upward gently to reposition the thread for the next stitch.

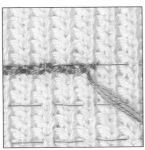

6. Repeat steps 2–5 across the row.

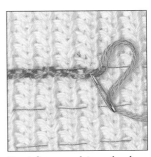

7. After working the last stitch, take the needle to the back through the hole in the knitted fabric halfway along the last stitch.

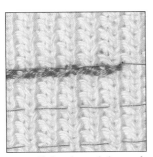

8. Pull the thread through and fasten off on the back of the fabric.

Trellis Stitch: **Two Step**

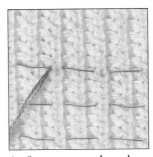

1. Secure your thread on the back of the knitted fabric. Bring it to the front on the left-hand side of the first knit stitch after the seam allowance.

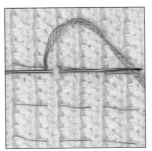

2. With the thread above the needle, take the needle from right to left behind the second half of the first knit stitch.

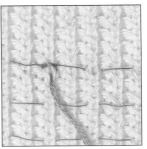

3. Pull the thread through.

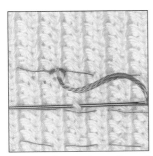

4. Keeping the thread above and the needle horizontal, take it from right to left behind the first half of the next knit stitch on the row below.

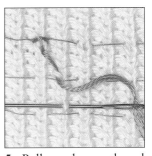 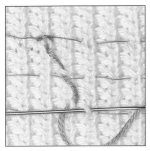 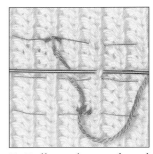 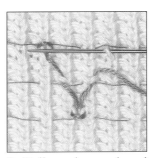

5. Pull the thread through. Keeping the thread above the needle, take it from right to left behind the second half of the knit stitch on the row below.

6. Pull the thread through. With the thread below the needle, take it from right to left through the first half of the next stitch on the same row.

7. Pull the thread through. Keeping thread below the needle, take it from right to left through the second half of the knit stitch on the row above.

8. Pull the thread through. Keeping the thread below the needle, take it from right to left through the first half of the next knit stitch on the row above.

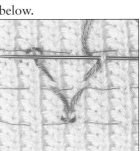 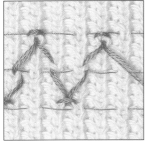 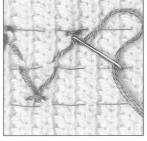 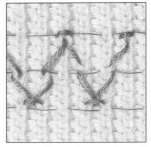

9. Pull the thread through. With the thread above the needle, take it from right to left through the second half of the knit stitch on the same row.

10. Repeat steps 3–9 across the row. Pull the thread through.

11. After working the last stitch (preferably a horizontal stitch), take the needle to the back through the hole in the knitted fabric halfway along the last stitch.

12. Pull the thread through fasten off on the back of the fabric.

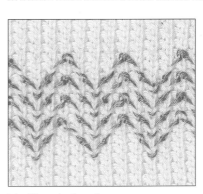 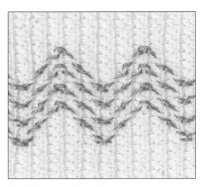 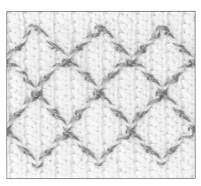

Trellis stitch—three step

Trellis stitch—four step

Trellis stitch—diamonds

Wave Stitch

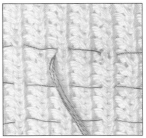 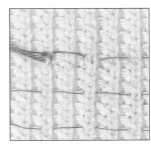 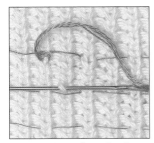

1. Secure your thread on the back of the knitted fabric. Bring it to the front on the left-hand side of the first knit stitch after the seam allowance.

2. With the thread above the needle, take the needle from right to left behind the second half of the first knit stitch.

3. Pull the thread through.

4. Keeping thread above and the needle horizontal, take it from right to left behind the first half of the next knit stitch the desired number of rows below.

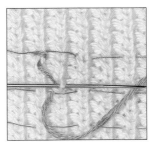 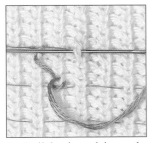 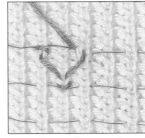 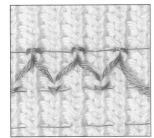

5. Pull the thread through. With the thread below the needle, take it from right to left behind the second half of the knit stitch.

6. Pull the thread through. Keeping the thread below the needle, take it from right to left behind the first half of the next knit stitch on the same row as the first used knit stitch.

7. Pull the thread through.

8. Repeat steps 2–7 across the row.

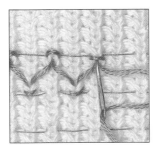 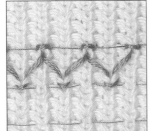 

9. After working the last stitch (preferably a horizontal stitch), take the needle to the back through the hole in the knitted fabric halfway along the last stitch.

10. Pull the thread through and fasten off on the back of the fabric.

The White Dove by Bernadette Janson

Finishing Techniques

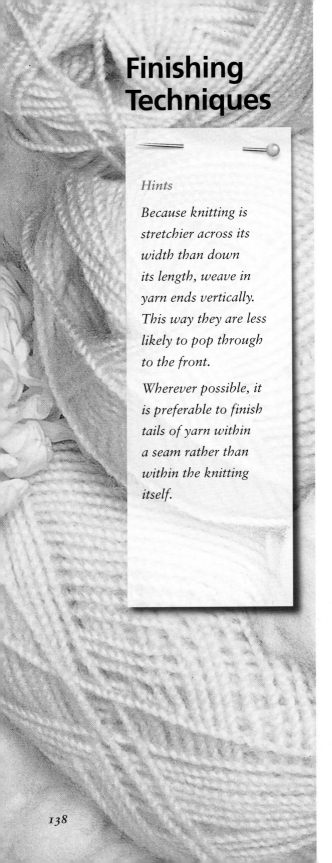

Hints

Because knitting is stretchier across its width than down its length, weave in yarn ends vertically. This way they are less likely to pop through to the front.

Wherever possible, it is preferable to finish tails of yarn within a seam rather than within the knitting itself.

Finishing Ends of Yarn

Finishing Ends of Yarn within a Seam

Use this method to finish off a tail of yarn whether you have used it to sew up the seam or not.

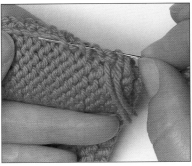

1. Thread the tail of yarn into a tapestry needle. Take the needle in and out of the edge stitches for approximately 1 1/2" (4 cm).

2. Pull the yarn through. Going in the opposite direction, take the needle in and out of the edge stitches for a distance slightly less than 1 1/2" (4 c m).

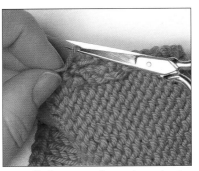

3. Pull the yarn through and trim the excess.

Finishing Ends of Yarn within the Knitting

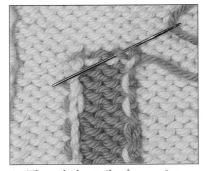

1. Thread the tail of yarn into a tapestry needle. On the back of the fabric, take the needle through the stitch next to the tail of yarn.

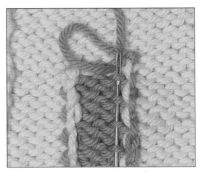

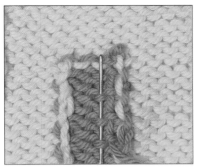

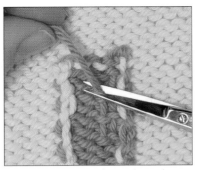

2. Pull the yarn through. Going vertically, take the needle in and out of the back of the stitches for approximately 1¹/₂" (4 cm). Do not take the needle through to the front of the fabric.

3. Pull the yarn through. Repeat step 2 in the opposite direction for a distance slightly less than 1¹/₂" (4 cm).

4. Pull the yarn through and trim the excess.

Always check the care instructions on the yarn label to see if you can apply steam to your knitting.

Blocking

Blocking is the key to a beautifully finished garment. It will also help the edges lie flat and make it easier to sew pieces together. You will need a blocking pad and long, rustproof, glass-headed pins or "T" pins. Blocking pads can be purchased from most needlework shops but you can also make your own by covering a large piece of styrofoam with cotton check fabric.

Place your knitted pieces face down on your blocking board and pin them out to the measurements stated in your pattern. Pin often so that you obtain nice, straight edges. Do not stretch ribbing; in fact, ribbed bands should not even need to be pinned.

Use one of the following methods to complete the blocking process:

- Place a damp cloth over the knitted piece. Press down lightly with your hands so that some of the moisture is released into the knitting. Leave it all to dry thoroughly.

- Place a pressing cloth over the knitting. Using a warm steam iron, move it around approximately ³/₈" to ³/₄" (1 to 2 cm) above the surface of the cloth until the steam has penetrated your knitting. Leave until dry.

- Place a damp pressing cloth over the knitting. Using a warm, dry iron and a press/lift action, gently cover the whole cloth. Do not drag the iron back and forth across the cloth. Leave until dry.

Sewing Up Seams
Ladder (a.k.a. Mattress) Stitch on Stockinette Stitch

Beginning a seam in this way prevents a little dip appearing at the lower end of the seam.

1. Thread the tail of yarn from your cast-on row and lay both pieces with right sides facing you. Take the needle from back to front through the corner stitch of the piece without the tail.

2. Pull the yarn through. Take the needle from back to front through the corner stitch on the opposite piece (the piece the tail is attached to). The yarn will form a sideways figure eight.

3. Pull the yarn firmly so that the two pieces lie close together. You are now ready to begin sewing your seam.

4. Take the needle under the horizontal bar between the first and second stitch in the first row on the right-hand piece.

5. Pull the yarn through. Take the needle under the horizontal bar between the first and second stitch in the first row on the left hand piece.

6. Pull the yarn through. Take the needle under the horizontal bar between the first and second stitch in the second row on the right hand piece.

7. Pull the yarn through. Take the needle under the horizontal bar between the first and second stitch in the second row on the left-hand piece.

8. Every four stitches pull the yarn firmly until the ladder stitches disappear. Continue in this manner to the end of the seam.

9. Fasten off the tails of yarn following the instructions on page 138. The seam is virtually invisible.

finishing techniques sewing up seams

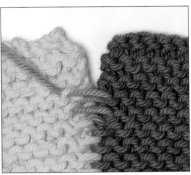

Ladder stitch on stockinette stitch variation

In this variation, the needle passes under two horizontal bars at a time.

Ladder stitch on reverse stockinette stitch

Alternate between working into the top loops on one side and the bottom loops on the other side.

Ladder stitch on garter stitch

Work in a similar manner to reverse stockinette stitch.

Back Stitch Back stitch creates a strong, firm seam.

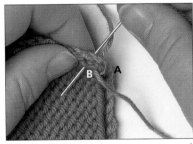

1. Place the two pieces right sides together with edges even. Leaving a 6" (15 cm) tail, bring the yarn to the front between the first and second stitches of both pieces (A).

2. Take the yarn around the end and through the same holes. Pull the yarn firmly.

3. Again take the yarn around the end. Bring it to the front at B, one knitting stitch farther along from A.

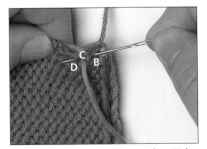

4. Pull the yarn through. Take the needle to the back at A and emerge at C, one knitting stitch farther along from B.

5. Pull the yarn through. Take the needle to the back at B and emerge at D, one knitting stitch farther along from C.

6. Pull the yarn through. Continue working to the end of the seam in exactly the same manner. Finish the ends of yarn following the instructions on page 138.

This technique is perfect for sewing up seams that you do not want to stretch out, such as shoulder seams.

sewing up seams finishing techniques

141

Overcast Stitch

1. Place the two pieces right sides together with edges even and knitting rows aligned. Leaving a 6" (15 cm) tail of yarn, bring the yarn to the front between the first and second stitches of both pieces (A).

2. Take the yarn over the edge and from back to front through exactly the same hole.

3. Pull the yarn through. Take the yarn over the edge and from back to front between the next pair of knots along the edge.

4. Pull the yarn through. Again take the yarn over the edge and from back to front between the next pair of knots along the edge.

5. Continue working to the end of the seam in exactly the same manner.

6. Finish the ends of yarn following the instructions on page 138.

finishing techniques sewing up seams

Hints

Use a tapestry needle for sewing seams. The blunt tip is less likely to split the yarn of the knitting stitches.

Do not pull stitches too tight because you will lose all elasticity from the seam.

It can be helpful to pin your knitted pieces together before working a back stitch seam.

Stitch seams with the yarn you used for knitting unless it is a particularly bulky yarn or one of the many uneven novelty yarns. In these instances, use a finer or smoother yarn that is as close as possible to the color of the yarn used for knitting. Ensure it also has the same care requirements.

Grafting
Grafting creates an invisible join between two pieces of knitting that have not been bound off. The sewn stitches look exactly the same as the knitted stitches. Keep the stitches on your needles and just slip off a few at a time as you work along the seam.

Grafting Stockinette Stitched Pieces

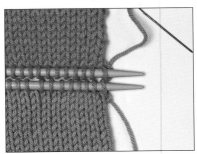

1. Place the two pieces close together with the right sides face up. Thread the tail of yarn on the upper piece into a needle.

2. Take the needle, from back to front, through the first stitch on the right hand side of the lower piece.

3. Pull the yarn through. Take the needle, from back to front, through the first stitch on the right-hand side of the upper piece.

4. Pull the yarn through and take the needle, from front to back, through the same stitch as before on the lower piece.

5. Pull the yarn through and take the needle, from back to front, through the next stitch to the left.

6. Pull the yarn through. Again, take the needle, from front to back, through the first stitch on the upper piece.

7. Pull the yarn through. Take the needle, from back to front, through the next stitch to the left.

8. Pull the yarn through. Repeat steps 4–7 to the end of the seam. Finish the ends of yarn following the instructions on page 138.

Hint

When grafting, ensure the yarn always goes through an "old" and a "new" stitch before moving to the other piece of knitting.

sewing up seams finishing techniques

143

Grafting Garter Stitched Pieces

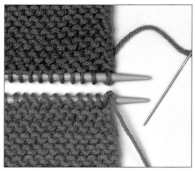

1. Place the two pieces close together with the right sides face up. Thread the tail of yarn on the upper piece into a needle.

2. Take the needle, from back to front, through the first stitch on the right-hand side of the lower piece.

3. Pull the yarn through. Take the needle, from front to back, through the first stitch on the right-hand side of the upper piece.

4. Pull the yarn through and take the needle, from front to back, through the same stitch as before on the lower piece.

5. Pull the yarn through and take the needle, from back to front, through the next stitch to the left.

6. Pull the yarn through. Again, take the needle, from back to front, through the first stitch on the upper piece.

7. Pull the yarn through. Take the needle, from front to back, through the next stitch to the left.

8. Pull the yarn through. Repeat steps 4–7 to the end of the seam. Finish the ends of yarn following the instructions on page 138.

Fringes, Pom-Poms, and Tassels

Fringes, pom-poms, and tassels can be a fabulous finishing touch to your knitted project.
They are easy to make and you can use either matching or contrasting yarns to great effect.

Fringes

1. Wrap the yarn around a rectangle of cardboard (or any other suitable object) that is a little longer than the length of the finished fringe you wish to make.

2. Using small, sharp scissors, cut all the pieces of yarn at one end.

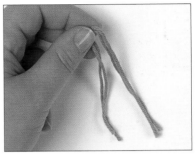

3. Pick up two to three lengths and fold them in half.

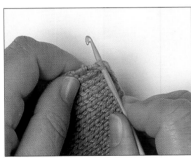

4. Take a crochet hook from front to back through the middle of a stitch in the first row of your knitting.

5. Hook the folded lengths of yarn and begin to pull them through the stitch. A loop will form.

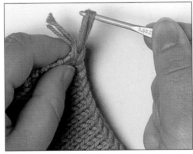

6. Hook the ends of the lengths of yarn and pull them through the loop.

7. Pull the ends firmly to secure the piece of fringe.

8. Repeat steps 3–7 across the row, attaching a piece of fringe through every second to fourth stitch. Trim the fringe so that it is even.

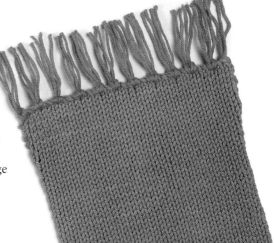

Pom-Poms

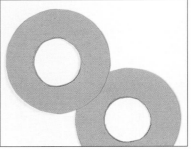

1. Cut two circles of cardboard slightly larger than the diameter of the finished pom-pom you wish to make. Make a hole in the center of each circle so that you have two doughnut shapes.

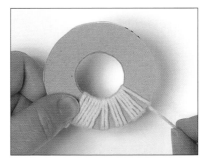

2. Place the two doughnut shapes together. Wrap the yarn through the hole and around the cardboard.

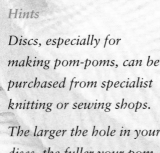

Hints

Discs, especially for making pom-poms, can be purchased from specialist knitting or sewing shops.

The larger the hole in your discs, the fuller your pom-pom will be. However, if your hole is too large, your pom-pom will end up oval shaped.

3. Continue wrapping until the shape is completely covered and the hole is filled. When the hole becomes small, take the yarn through it with a tapestry needle.

4. Using a pair of small, sharp scissors, cut the yarn around the edge by sliding the blade of the scissors between the two pieces of cardboard.

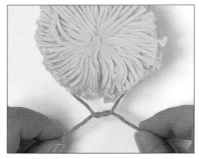

5. Slightly separate the two pieces of cardboard. Take a length of yarn between the cards and tie in a firm knot. Leave a long enough tail to fasten the pom-pom to your garment.

6. Remove the cardboard circles and fluff out the pom-pom.

Tassels

The following instructions are for a very simple and soft tassel.

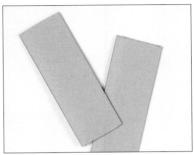

1. Cut two rectangles of cardboard slightly longer than the length of the finished tassel you wish to make.

2. Place the two rectangles together. Wrap the yarn from end to end around the cardboard.

3. Continue wrapping until the yarn around the cardboard is the desired thickness.

4. Thread a length of yarn into a tapestry needle. Take the needle between the two pieces of cardboard.

5. Pull both ends of the yarn to the top and tie loosely around the wraps.

6. Using a pair of small, sharp scissors, cut the yarn around the opposite edge by sliding the blade of the scissors between the two pieces of cardboard.

7. Remove the cardboard. Firmly retie the yarn around the wraps. Wrap and tie a second length of yarn around the tassel at least 3/8" (1 cm) below the tied end.

8. Thread the ends of this length of yarn into a tapestry needle. Take them through the center of the tassel and to the bottom.

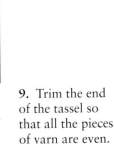

9. Trim the end of the tassel so that all the pieces of yarn are even.

fringes, pom-poms, and tassels finishing techniques

147

Caring for Knitted Garments

Laundering

Always follow the instructions on the yarn care label and never leave a knitted garment to soak.

If your piece is machine washable, use your washing machine's gentle cycle and do not have the water too warm. Use a detergent specially designed for woolen garments.

To hand wash, place your garment in tepid water with a small amount of mild detergent. Gently squeeze the water through your garment. Rinse thoroughly to remove all traces of the detergent. Squeeze out as much water as possible. Spread out a colorfast towel in a shady spot and lay your garment on it to dry.

Some yarns can be dry-cleaned. If this is the case with your garment, ask the dry cleaner not to press it or hang it on a coat hanger.

Storing

Store knitted pieces on a shelf or in a drawer away from sunlight. If you hang them they are likely to stretch out of shape. Protect your knitted garments from insects by using a commercial moth repellent or lavender or cedar shavings.

Hints

Make your own care label and sew it into your knitted garment. This way you do not have to rely on your memory for how to wash a particular garment. Write the care instructions onto a piece of cotton tape or ribbon with a permanent fabric marker.

Never wring the water from a knitted garment. You will distort it and can matt the fibers.

If a loop of yarn is snagged, carefully ease it back along the row with the tip of a needle, until it disappears and all stitches are back to their original size.

Lengthening and Shortening Knitted Garments

If your garment grows—or you do—it is quite a simple matter to adjust the length.

Lengthening

1. Using small needles, pick up the fronts of the stitches above and below the position at which you wish to lengthen the garment, leaving two rows of knitting between the needles.

2. Cut across the knitting between the two needles.

3. Remove the yarn from the cut edges back to each knitting needle.

4. Knit across the top of the bottom piece using the same size needles as the garment was originally knitted with.

5. Continue working rows until you have added the required length.

6. Join the two pieces of knitting together following the instructions for grafting on pages 143–144.

Shortening

1. Using small needles, pick up the fronts of the stitches above and below the position at which you wish to shorten the garment.

2. Cut the first stitch in the row just below the upper needle.

3. Using a tapestry needle, pull out the first row of stitches.

4. Unravel the remaining rows down to the lower knitting needle.

5. Join the two pieces of knitting together following the instructions for grafting on pages 143–144.

Hint

When picking up stitches, use knitting needles that are a size or two smaller than those originally used to knit the garment.

caring for knitted garments finishing techniques

149

index